Praise for *Where I End*

Having lived with quadriplegia for more than fifty years, I've heard a great many stories about people who have suffered life-altering injuries. But some rise above the rest—perhaps it's the skill in storytelling, or how this person becomes a precious friend with every chapter. It's how I feel about the book you hold in your hands. Kate Clark understands pain and loss like few do, but is able to share that in an impossibly winsome, personal way. I give *Where I End* my strong recommendation, and who knows? This Spirit-inspired story may even alter your life before you turn the last page.

JONI EARECKSON TADA
Joni and Friends International Disability Center

Kate Clark is one of the most remarkable people I have ever met. She is also one of the best writers and all that she is and all that she has been through is told so well in *Where I End*. Her story will inspire you to hang on to God when the unexpected tragedy strikes you. It will reveal how anyone can get through anything by trusting God, and doing whatever you can to move forward. There are tears from Kate's story born out of loss and the joy of a new life found. Read this book. You will not be disappointed and you will not be the same when you are finished.

STEVE ARTERBURN
Founder of New Life Ministries and Women of Faith

Where I End shook me to the core and left me on my knees in worship. Many theologians can write sound doctrine, but few can write it as beautifully as Kate Clark has done. Her elegant prose, courageous vulnerability, spritely humor, and profound insights take us deep into a narrative of fearsome suffering and godly perseverance. Any Christian trying to find God's face in the midst of hardship needs to read this book. Clark's story reminds us that only when we reach our end do we truly discover where Jesus Christ begins.

BRYAN M. LITFIN
Professor of Theology, Moody Bible Institute

Katherine Elizabeth Clark says, "I will not try to explain suffering." She stays true to her words. What she does instead is show us what suffering looks like, the kind of suffering that happens when something gets broken amid children on a playground, and that something is you. But in addition, she shows us what resilience looks like, what the Christian calls "hope." What this woman and wife and mother and daughter and friend discovers is that so much depends upon the Son of Man, hanging on a cross, embracing fully a great sadness, but also the beautiful grace of God.

JOHN BLASE
Author of *The Jubilee* and *Know When to Hold 'Em: The High Stakes Game of Fatherhood*

A single tragic moment altered the course of Katherine Clark's life. *Where I End* is a story about that moment, but also about so much more. Clark writes with grace, depth, candor, and maturity about her difficult journey toward both healing and acceptance of her new life. *Where I End* offers powerful insight about the nature of discipleship for anyone who has found that their life has taken a turn into uncharted territory.

MICHELLE VAN LOON
Speaker, blogger, and author of the forthcoming *Born to Wander: Recovering Our Pilgrim Identity*

In what she calls her "horrible wonderful" story, Kate Clark refuses to sentimentalize suffering or to bring false closure to the potentially tragic event that changed hers and her family's lives forever. Instead, she offers the reader the unexpected: an unclichéd account colored with sensory, lively writing laced with touches of humor and whimsy, girded with theology, and embedded in the hope that Christ, not circumstances, offers.

ROSALIE DE ROSSET
Professor of Communications and Literature, Moody Bible Institute

This book is for those who suffer and those who care for the suffering; in other words, this book is for all of us. Within a great constellation of Scripture, theologians, and storytellers, Clark gives language to what increases our suffering and what eases our suffering. Clark's gentle movement between her story of pain and her wisdom about that pain reminds us of God's movements of grace in the midst of suffering.

NICOLE MAZZARELLA
Associate Professor of English, Wheaton College; author of *This Heavy Silence*, a Christy Award–winning novel, and winner of the 2006 Christianity Today Book Award for fiction

Kate's story stirs me as a mother and wife, a physician, and a Christian. While it is a story of healing, it is even more a story of a daily walk with Christ through suffering. Throughout the telling, she references other beloved stories and ultimately points us to the greatest story and, in doing so, gives us a glimpse of suffering imbued with beauty, dignity, and hope.

MARTHA MCGRAW
Neurologist, Northwestern Medicine

Where I End

A STORY OF TRAGEDY, TRUTH, AND REBELLIOUS HOPE

Katherine Elizabeth Clark

MOODY PUBLISHERS

CHICAGO

Edited by Pamela Joy Pugh
Interior design: Erik M. Peterson
Author photo: Michael Hudson Photography
Cover design: Connie Gabbert Design and Illustration
Cover photo of field and landscape copyright (c) 2017 by Triff/Shutterstock (176193992). All rights reserved.

Library of Congress Cataloging-in-Publication Data

Names: Clark, Katherine Elizabeth, author.
Title: Where I end : a story of tragedy, truth, and rebellious hope /
    Katherine Elizabeth Clark.
Description: Chicago : Moody Publishers, 2018. | Includes bibliographical
    references.
Identifiers: LCCN 2017040146 (print) | LCCN 2017047170 (ebook) | ISBN
    9780802496348 | ISBN 9780802416834
Subjects: LCSH: Consolation. | Suffering--Religious aspects–Christianity. |
    Accident victims--Religious life. | Accident victims—United States. |
    Clark, Katherine Elizabeth.
Classification: LCC BV4905.3 (ebook) | LCC BV4905.3 .C533 2018 (print) | DDC
    277.3092 [B] —dc23
LC record available at https://lccn.loc.gov/2017040146

We hope you enjoy this book from Moody Publishers. Our goal is to provide high-quality, thought-provoking books and products that connect truth to your real needs and challenges. For more information on other books and products written and produced from a biblical perspective, go to www.moodypublishers.com or write to:

Moody Publishers
820 N. LaSalle Boulevard
Chicago, IL 60610

1 3 5 7 9 10 8 6 4 2

Printed in the United States of America

~ for John

A promise is a bold thing. Little did we know
the audaciousness of our pledge to love each other
forever—no matter what—until we found ourselves
in the wreckage. I knew I had a good man but did not
know how very good until we met in this crucible.

~ and for William and Gwyneth

You are the joy and love of the promise made so
many years ago. May you always know in the
very fiber of your being the great love the Lord has
for you and His power to keep you through every
trial and tribulation—He is always the way home.

CONTENTS

THE STORY

Why would anyone write a book about herself? It could be perceived as a bit self-involved. To be sure, bookstores possess profound stories written by brave storytellers. The sober author, however, is well aware that her tale might slip from something beautiful and life-giving to mere vainglory. At least, that is a fear of mine.

I live a fairly simple, quiet life, which I love. To the extent that I'm able, I live my life offline. I don't blog or use Facebook as my everyday life isn't, for the most part, all that fascinating; and I know there are far finer sages than I. So why have I devoted a season to composing this work?

My husband is a college professor. And when he was the newcomer on campus, he was asked to speak to the faculty and staff—to share some background history, an illustrative vignette about himself. On the 5:00 a.m. commute into the Windy City, before the sun could rout the darkness, he told a fellow professor that he wasn't sure if he was going to share *the story*. His friend was confounded. "You have to tell the story," he insisted. "The only faithful response to living this story is to tell it."

So in an effort to honor the triune God of the gospel, be He ever blessed, I have penned what I remember as best I can recall it. I have written and rewritten this story in my head. Yet the task of putting it to paper has proved more formidable than I imagined it would be. I have jilted this project several times, not wanting to revisit the gruesome details of the past or simply feeling inadequate to put into words an event that continues to shape my family.

Strictly speaking, this not an autobiography, nor is it a piece of journalism about a particular event. Rather, it is a series of reflections—broadly but not strictly chronological—in the wake of an event that has shaped my story as well as the stories of those who love me.

Ultimately, this is a tale about God's faithfulness to a fragile young woman—a story that speaks loudly of a God, the one true God, who confounds the wisdom of mankind and heals when doctors cannot.

PART ONE

the fall

1

"Yes, well, I am crippled," said Madame LaVaughn, "and that, I assure you, goes somewhat beyond sadness."

—Kate DiCamillo, *The Magician's Elephant*

I have a story to tell. A tale penned in grief and sorrow. But it is also a story abounding in hope, beauty, and the miraculous. It is at times humiliating.

And although this tale has a good end, I must warn you, it is by no means a fairy-tale ending, which simply is to say that this story is real. For in fairy tales the girl always finds her true love, good defeats evil, and everyone is happy! But I have not found such wide-eyed optimism to be the substance of our lives.

In this life on earth, sadly, the girl does not always find her true love. Evil capriciously swallows men, women, and children in its path. And on this side of heaven, a shadow looms over even the brightest of our joys.

Unlike fiction, however, true stories have a power all their own. And in spite of its painful and grotesque underpinnings

—or perhaps because of them—my narrative is, above all things, amazing.

Now, I feel the need to clarify at the start that *I* am not amazing. Did you think this was an epic tale of a mighty heroine? Let me put that erroneous thought to rest. *I* am full of flaws and sharp edges. I am half Irish, and my husband likes to tell people that I am among the Fighting Irish. As you can imagine, a fighting disposition regretfully clashes with the harmony of a family at times; it is, however, helpful, perhaps essential, when catastrophe threatens to upend and best one's life. But I am getting ahead of myself. Let us begin at the beginning.

My story commences on a Friday. And I think we can agree this is a very good day to start a story. I awoke with that peculiar joy, that little heartfelt bliss that wells up inside you when you sleepily realize today is not just any day— today is *Friday*. Friday means I survived the week. Friday dangles the hope of a little extra weekend sleep and some family time traipsing through woodlands, meandering in the open air. And this Friday was brimming with possibilities.

To begin with, Grand Rapids, Michigan, was awash in late spring sunshine. For the past several months, we had a visitor—a blustery guest—who had gifted our doorsteps with almost one hundred inches of snow. The great thaw had led to a small-scale flood in the lower level of our rented duplex, and I was just beginning to feel "dry." So to me, this May sun was like a long-lost friend. And like any true friend, the sunshine entered our home with no need of invitation, filling our rooms, our very cores, with its spritely warmth.

My heart was full, as was my happy agenda for Friday, May 29, 2009. Now, if I had authored the day's events, they would have gone something like this:

1. Eat breakfast as a family with my husband, John, our seven-year-old son William, and our daughter Gwyneth, four years of age.
2. Escort William to school.
3. Prepare a dish for the last teachers' appreciation luncheon of the school year, and prepare dinner for our evening date with friends.
4. Read some poems or a book during lunch to William's first grade class.
5. Enjoy the afternoon spring breeze with Gwyneth; perhaps we could discover some wildflowers, late-blooming tulips, or tadpoles.
6. Dine with some sweet friends. I was especially looking forward to seeing our former neighbors. The youngest of the four children, Ava, age five, and Ethan, three, had practically lived at our house during the year we were neighbors. Outgoing, merry, and always entertaining—they were so easy to love.

This was the cheerful Friday I'd envisioned.

William asked if he could ride his bike to school, so I laced up my well-worn tennis shoes. I didn't grab the jogger stroller because Gwyneth decided to stay home with her daddy. The trek was not so far, but it seemed a good opportunity to sneak in a quick run. William, like a young racehorse out of the gate, boldly led the way through the dewy grass and onto the sidewalk.

I attempted to keep pace with my speedy first grader, and he regularly glanced back grinning cheekily, slightly taunting me. Keeping pace a short distance behind the treads of his red Schwinn, I belted out the Beatles' "Here Comes the Sun," the first tune on a mix of songs playing quietly on my MP3 player. William laughed and insisted I stop. I caught my boy at the intersection. We paused briefly on the curb until the WALK signal bellowed, commanding us to cross. Together William and I ventured into the street. This space always made me nervous.

I felt relief after we safely navigated the busy intersection, and I pushed again to keep pace with the boy on the express bicycle. When we finally reached the school, I waited. The start bell hummed to the children, urging them to make some sense of their makeshift lines and ready themselves for the day. I reminded William I'd be back soon. I watched his backpack disappear through the school doors, cranked up my music, and ran straight home—no time for detours or extra miles today.

The morning was a blur of activity. After my shower, Gwyneth and I put our culinary talents to work, which resulted in a black bean salsa dish and a packed lunch. I assured John that I'd be back soon to attend to the kitchen and hoped he wouldn't discover the empty cans and cutting boards littering the counter. I stuffed the brown bag and a true-or-false book about pets into my satchel, grabbed the salsa and tortilla chips, and boomeranged back to Will's school, this time via our green Volkswagen Golf with my four-year-old friend in tow.

So far, no big changes to the day's plans. Gwyneth and I had ventured to school at eleven o'clock each Friday morning all school year long. This was a tradition we both loved. Gwyneth would share her big brother's desk and eat lunch with the class, while I'd read stories and poems. This gave William's teacher a much deserved break, and us an opportunity to visit our William. We knew all the toothy grins, the wild and mild personalities in Mr. Wright's spirited class. And our affable Gwyneth was deeply loved among the first graders.

But today was particularly significant because it marked the end to our tradition. This was the last full Friday of the school year, so we had to bid farewell to story time with our impish friends.

I think we were both feeling a little gloomy about saying goodbye—I know I was—so after lunch we stayed for recess. My budding entomologist William disappeared into an open grassy field far beyond the school building in search of anything that hopped, buzzed, or crawled. Both Will and his sister have inherited their dad's hawklike vision. Drop any of them in a park or forest and within minutes, they will point out toads, frogs, praying mantises, fish, or any number of birds. I do not possess this visual gift. Gwyneth and I decided to savor the brilliant sunshine on the playground. The swings called to my dear girl, so she cajoled one of her favorite friends, first-grader Mia, into pushing her. With each good-natured little shove from Mia, Gwyneth rhythmically ascended higher, kissing the sky with her toes. Oh, the joy of swinging. I can still picture Mia's rich dark skin, giant-sized dandelion puffed pigtails, and larger-than-life smile.

Sydnie and Amea, the two little girls hanging on me, responded enthusiastically to my suggestion of a game of tag. Before I knew it, we were whirling about the playground. Now, if you've ever braved a round of tag as an adult with a group of kids, you know that before long, you're the only one being chased—even the kids who aren't "It" are chasing you. Despite these odds, not to mention my jean skirt and flip-flops, I was doing a pretty good job of avoiding the growing kite string of children close at my heels.

Unbeknownst to me, precisely as our game was getting underway, a boy was scaling a large jungle gym full of tubes and slides. He navigated his way to the peak of the play structure where there were three slide options: a fast slide, a bumpy slide, or a zigzag slide. On this day at this time, however, the boy was not tempted by the cascading purple slopes. Instead, he had a different, quite ill-fated idea; he climbed over the protective barrier atop the edifice. Light and jaunty, I was running. I was feeling victorious, defeating these kids at their own little game. And just as I jetted near the slides,

he

bounded

into the air

and

crashed

onto my head.

My neck cracked under the weight of his sneakers—snapping like a whip forward and abruptly back. My agile, sure, and steady frame stopped short, wobbled ever so briefly, and went limp. Entangled together, the boy and I thudded onto the ground.

His elbow: fractured.

I: paralyzed from the neck down.

2

Holding firmly to the trunk, I took a step toward him,
and then my knees bent and I jounced the limb. Finny,
his balance gone, swung his head around to look at me for
an instant with extreme interest, and then he tumbled
sideways, broke through the little branches below
and hit the bank with a sickening, unnatural thud.

—John Knowles, *A Separate Peace*

The cheerful rollicking playground noise was pierced by screams of a different sort. Frightened and pained voices now shattered the sweet air: the boy on top of me was repeatedly hollering, "My aaarrmm is broken! My aaarrmm is broken!" And in crazy high-pitched panic, one of my tag chasers, a little girl, simultaneously shrieked, "Get . . . off . . . of . . . her!"

Immobile in the woodchips, I lay on my back, one flip-flop on, one off. The wailing boy was lifted off me and whisked to the office. A crowd of curious children began to form a makeshift circle around my body. Mrs. Bratt, a second grade teacher whom I did not know personally, was soon kneeling at my side, leaning directly over me. Stunned and not a little shocked, I confessed in a wavering voice, "I can't move."

She began to pray, and I too was now silently begging God, *Please do not let me be paralyzed. Please do not let me be paralyzed.* The crowd of children pressed and continued to multiply. Someone spoke into the nightmare, explaining to the nervous elementary kids that I was just resting. My sweet Gwyneth knew better. She bolted from the circle, entrusting her feet to find her big brother in the wide-open field behind the school. The little girl who'd been right on my heels in the game of tag must have had the same idea as she arrived just moments before Gwyneth. Tears spilled down her face as she bid William to come, his mom was hurt. More kids descended on Will. They declared, "Your mom is dead." Bewildered, William suspected trickery. With feline caution and suspicion, he made his way to the playground woodchips. When they reached the logjam of kids, William and Gwyneth blended silently into the mass, two more faces in a crowd whose nearness I sensed but could not see.

Whistles began to blow. And the freedom and frolic of recess was cut short. The pressing crowds were ushered in lines against the brick building with gray siding. Children began to cry (I think because they knew something strangely horrible had happened and not because recess was prematurely scrubbed—maybe it was both), teachers began to cry.

And though it was not a Christian school, many began to pray, including my little friends from Mr. Wright's class.

I don't know how much time had elapsed, but I had been splayed on the ground far too long for my liking. Everyone around me waited, hoped, prayed for me to rise under my own power. It was like that moment in a football stadium when a player is injured; everyone is holding their breath, and when the athlete rises, a collective sigh of relief comes, followed by cheers and applause. But I could not even feel my limbs, let alone call them to action. "I need an ambulance," I weakly confided to the teacher.

My husband was clicking laptop keys in the lower level of our duplex, engrossed in his doctoral dissertation. A father who happened to be at the school dialed my home number and held his cellphone to my ear. I heard my voice on the answering machine and after the beep, implored my husband to pick up the phone. I was not panicked, nor was I crying. But I told John I was hurt, that he needed to come right away. I remembered that I had the car at school, but a close friend was now at my side. I informed John, "Rachelle is coming to get you." He left his dissertation midsentence, a project that little did he know, would not be revisited for many, many, many months.

The incandescent sun, no longer friend, tormented me with its direct and unforgiving glow. I gazed—I had no choice—into its hot light. It blurred my vision; the white star beamed brightly on my pain, untroubled and carefree.

William's teacher was at my side, grief in his eyes. I beseeched him to track down Gwyneth. She had been taken inside the school and given a book to read. My fierce four-year-old was angry and confused. She wanted to help, yet we were both helpless. William was now with his class, also dazed. No words had been spoken between my children and me.

John arrived at the school, followed by an ambulance and paramedics. He came to me first—calm, with a reassuring, almost bright, look on his face; then he searched for our kids. He found them severely shaken and prayed with them.

A small crowd of adults remained around me. A paramedic knelt by my side and introduced himself as Jeremy. I suddenly saw my arm suspended in the air, held high not of my own will or power but by the paramedic. He removed his grip, and I watched as my arm flopped unnaturally, powerless against the force of gravity. Jeremy caught my awkward limb just before it collided with the woodchips. In that moment, my steady world, where bodies work in harmony with brains, was bartered for an unrecognizable universe, something resembling a Salvador Dalí painting; I felt as if I had slipped into a surreal, disorientated dream.

My heart began to pump rapidly—with blood and fear. I felt the panic coursing through my veins.

"Can you feel this?"

"No."

"Can you feel this?"

"No."

Jeremy gave instructions. I was carefully rolled onto a board, my neck placed in a brace. When my body was securely in place, the paramedics adeptly carried me across the playground and lifted me into the ambulance. John left our two crying children to join the paramedics and me—he climbed into the front seat of the ambulance. The sirens blared as we made our way through the city, more noise disrupting the bright spring sky.

I arrived at the hospital emergency room naked—my clothes had been cut off in the ambulance. Over the next couple of months, I would see the paramedic Jeremy and tell him that he owed me a jean skirt. I still haven't found its equal. It was the first of many losses, but certainly not the gravest. But I digress. Doctors and nurses surrounded me, flooded me with questions. I was turned this way, and flipped that way. Poked. Prodded. I felt nothing. Well, not quite nothing. What I felt was an enormous weight upon me, an immense pressure, as if someone was stacking bricks on top of bricks. I could not move my body because it was pinned beneath a medieval torture press.

"Are you a runner?" the emergency doctor asked.

"Yes, I run a little. I ran this morning."

"Do you smoke?"

"No."

"Can you feel this?"

Feel what? "No."

But I did start to sense intense pain building in my body. My brain, discerning something was amiss, began to send pain signals. My nerves were on fire.

Following the emergency overhaul, I was placed in a small holding room. A nurse placated my parched tongue with some ice chips. When my kids arrived, the deadness of my limbs hit me afresh. I could not comfort William or Gwyneth with a hug. I could not find comfort in hugging them.

Oh, Lord, I long to put my arms around my son and my daughter.

William had a stack of papers, notes of encouragement from his classmates. He attempted to hand them to me, but through a pained and awkward exchange realized I could not reach for them. Apologetically, he began to sort the pictures one by one, holding them for me to see, then stacking them on top of me. The leaves of paper, light as air, slid off my body but the medieval press bore down, tightening its grip unrelentingly on my chest. A hospital worker entered the room and told us the emergency room doctor had sent orders for me to have an MRI. My dear William, longing to find a place in a world turned upside-down, was cut short.

I spent the next hour in the elongated claustrophobia-inducing tube, feeling surprisingly calm and praying persistently. I prayed for healing, for relief from the ever-increasing pressure on my body. *Lord, I want to hug my children. I want to run alongside my kids. I want to braid Gwyneth's hair. Please, Lord, let this cup pass from me.*

I was wheeled into another holding room to wait. John was hopeful. This is probably just a stinger, right? As college football fans, we'd watched players take a hit to the head, collapse, and lie stunned, immobile in the grass. Eventually, the numbness or weakness resulting from the powerful blow would subside, and soon after, the athlete would be back on the field—worst-case scenario, he'd be out for the duration of the game.

Yet when the ER doctor returned with the test results, John and I immediately perceived the answer from his grave and ashen expression—all hope had drained from his face. This was no nerve-pinched stinger. My spinal cord, he explained, was crushed and lacerated. I needed emergency surgery. He informed us that they were looking for a surgeon willing and able to perform the operation.

Phone calls to family and friends followed this gauntlet of information, as we had no family residing in Grand Rapids.

As many loved ones began their heavy-hearted journey to the west side of Michigan, the surgeon arrived. Initially, on seeing my MRI results, this surgeon said he needed some time to think about whether or not he wanted to take on this operation. The injury was dangerously high, at C3, the third cervical vertebra in my neck.

I liked the look of him. There was no pretense. He told us that I had suffered a Christopher Reeve–level injury, not only dangerously high but gravely serious. He explained that he needed to make a cut across the front of my neck, remove the disc crushing my spinal cord, and put my spine back together by fusing together my third, fourth, and fifth vertebrae (C3, C4, and C5) with some donor bone.

My parents arrived, having made the nearly three-hour drive and, upon seeing my mom, I felt once again like a small child; all those moments of vulnerability and fear, the searing pain of freshly skinned knees, of cuts and stitches, collectively converged on my heart. I wanted to be brave, but I found myself needing to fight back tears. I was wheeled into surgery about the same time we should have been arriving to see our friends for dinner. Oh, someone should call them.

3

There are three necessary prayers and they have
three words each. They are these, "Lord have mercy.
Thee I adore. Into Thy hands." Not difficult to remember.
If in times of distress you hold to these you will do well.

—Elizabeth Goudge, *The Scent of Water*

As the hospital staff began the heavy task of surgery—sedating, inserting breathing tubes, cutting through flesh, evaluating, deliberating, carefully removing broken or damaged fragments, fusing bones and metal, stitching skin back together—friends, family, and teachers gathered in the hospital waiting room, trickling in throughout the evening. William's former prekindergarten teacher played a game of cards with him and his sister. The mother of the boy who jumped on me remained off to the side; her son was in surgery at the same time as I was to fix his shattered elbow.

We are fragile creatures—a truth suppressed or forgotten, but within the waiting room crucible, we are reacquainted

with the frailty of our lives. In his book *A Grief Observed*,
C. S. Lewis wrote,

> God has not been trying an experiment on my faith
> or love in order to find out their quality. He knew it
> already. It was I who didn't. In this trial He makes us
> occupy the dock, the witness box, and the bench all at
> once. He always knew that my temple was a house of
> cards. His only way of making me realize the fact was
> to knock it down.[1]

Our temples are houses of cards, collapsing with the
smallest brush of a hand, the slightest puff of air. We are
depending on a job, our health, a child, our marriage, a
retirement fund—yet, in a breath, all can be lost. In the
hospital waiting room, or whenever we acknowledge our
great need, some form of the prayer *Lord have mercy. Thee I
adore. Into Thy hands,* finds itself on our lips. In our distress,
we either find solace by remembering who we need and to
whom we belong, or we choose the path of despair, refusing
to be gathered into the arms of the Father.

We either seek His kind face or deny ourselves His comfort.

A prayer for favor, adoration, and trust began on the
playground woodchips. It was uttered by friends and family
in some form or another in the hospital waiting room. This
prayer would become the heartbeat of my broken life over
the next days, months, year. It still today endures.

4

Using the hospital Care Page online community site, a friend started an account the night of my surgery in order to keep family and friends updated. Below is the first of many posts.

Care Page Update
Posted May, 2009 11:53 p.m.

Kate is out of surgery and has been moved to the ICU. The surgeon reported that the surgery went well, and he was able to remove the disc in the fourth vertebra as planned. This was done in order to give the spinal cord the room it needs to swell. The doctor also removed an unexpected bone spur that should not have been there. Significant damage was done to the spinal cord on impact, and the MRI that was performed earlier in the day showed obvious injury. The surgeon could not give a prognosis at this point. He likened Kate's injury to that of Christopher Reeve, which will require a lengthy recovery period. This could mean possibly six to eighteen months of rehabilitation, most likely at Mary Free Bed Rehabilitation Hospital. Kate's breathing will be closely monitored to assess her ability to breathe on her own. If not, she will need a breathing tube indefinitely. Although this is difficult news to hear, the family remains hopeful that God will work a miracle.

For those of you who don't know how this occurred, Kate caught the fall of a child from a high piece of playground equipment. Kate was playing tag with several kids at lunch recess when a child fell on top of her. The boy broke his arm, which required surgery, and he is currently staying at the same hospital.

More news will be available tomorrow. Thanks for your prayers and concern.

Sincerely,

Leslie

5

Vanity and pride are different things, though the words are often used synonymously. A person may be proud without being vain. Pride relates more to our opinion of ourselves, vanity to what we would have others think of us.

—Jane Austen, *Pride and Prejudice*

I love the distinction Austen makes between vanity and pride. I wish that I could proudly (yes, I jest) separate and exempt myself from one of these vices. Sadly, I am guilty of both. In fact, on the playground just before those sneakers collided with my head, a thought flirting with both pride and vanity flitted through my brain.

Lying helpless in my hospital bed as time went on, I could not but wonder if this deadly simple thought is what put into motion the events that followed—the precise timing of the boy's jump and my placement near the jungle gym. Was I struck down, smitten by God? I can honestly say I was not afflicted with the question, "Why *me*?" However, I was harassed, at times, by the question, "Why?"

You are likely familiar with the story of Job in the Bible, which I will revisit in greater detail later. News of numerous and terrible tragedies of Job spread. And three friends, not wanting Job to bear his pain alone, came and simply sat with him in his sorrow for a week. "No one spoke a word to him, for they saw his suffering was very great" (Job 2:13). After the beautiful silence of these friends, however, the "why" question reared its head. Trying to make sense of the death and loss, Job's friends wrongly concluded that he was being punished for some sin.

I was, like Job's friends, tempted to wonder if indeed I was being punished. Verses in Proverbs haunted me from time to time.

> When pride comes, then comes disgrace, but with the humble is wisdom. (11:2)
>
> Pride goes before destruction, and a haughty spirit before a fall. (16:18)

Oooh, that second one had a particular sting. Now, I could rightly claim that everyone wrestles with vanity or pride. The logical conclusion could therefore follow that under God's righteous judgment none would be left standing. Despite its truth, this line of thought was not a comfort to me.

I cannot embrace our American notion of fairness, as I do not think that in order to be "fair" God is obligated to treat everyone the same. Many years ago when I was auditing a seminary class, a professor posed a question that remained fastened to me: "Whatever made you think that God is fair?" he challenged. Righteous, to be sure; just, most certainly; holy, absolutely; but "fair"?—well, not according to our standards. This professor pointed out how God gives lavishly to some and not to others. He blesses some with extraordinary musical talent while others cannot carry a tune. To some He gives a brilliant mind while others struggle to make out the simplest arithmetic problems. He gives great wealth to a few, while others live humbly, trusting God for their daily bread.

And He can give and take, dear friends, precisely because He's God. We do not naturally or readily love the idea of God being God. In fact, the temptation to question God's wisdom, love, and authority harkens back to the beginning. The plot is eerily familiar, is it not? In the third chapter of Genesis, we find Eve in a deadly conversation. The serpent strikes with the query: "Did God actually say, 'You shall not eat of any tree in the garden'?" (v. 1). After Eve's fumbling and failing to get the answer correct, he continues with his inquiry:

> The serpent said to the woman, "You will not surely die. For God knows that when you eat of it your eyes will be opened, and you will be like God, knowing good and evil." (vv. 4–5)

How dare God keep this fruit from me? That's all it took. In the recesses of our hearts we all think we're a little wiser, a bit more compassionate, a measure more loving than He. We think, *If I were God, I would not have allowed that to happen. If I were God, I would have rescued those people. If God is kind and good, He would give to me what He's given to my far less deserving neighbor.* We surreptitiously intimate that we are benevolent givers while He is miserly.

Nowhere in Scripture does anyone praise God for being "fair." But there is ever so much about Him being just. He is indeed the champion of justice. We must lean heavily on this truth when faced with the realities of this world. Our hearts long for the defeat of evil, for truth to ring above the din of deceit, for life to swallow up death, for beauty to put ugliness to flight.

We long for what is broken to be made right. For the weak to be loved. The lost to be rescued. The wayward to be redeemed. We long for the truth, goodness, and beauty of Jesus to be manifested in our lives and the lives of the people around us.

Scripture repeatedly proclaims that God is love. Our hearts long for His love to be boldly reflected in our lives. A love that is true, good, faithful, joyful, unsullied, unchanging, and unceasing. This love is evidenced solely in and through God the Father, Son, and Holy Spirit.

So what does this have to do with my vanity, pride, and subsequent fall? The "why?" question is a dark labyrinth. Any conclusions I might come to would be presumptuous. The disciples found themselves in this quicksand. When they inwardly asked themselves why a tower crushed eighteen people, they came to the seemingly obvious conclusion of guilt. The people lying dead in the debris had sinned and been judged by a righteous God. Jesus knows what they're thinking, and He calls them on it.

> Those eighteen on whom the tower in Siloam fell and killed them: do you think that they were worse offenders than all the others who lived in Jerusalem? No, I tell you; but unless you repent, you will all likewise perish. (Luke 13:4–5)

I do not and cannot know the answer to "Why did I fall?" this side of heaven, perhaps ever. Yet, that doesn't mean that I cannot ask questions. The psalms are laden with the gut-wrenchingly honest pleas of those who are suffering. God has no trouble bearing up under my inquiries. There are questions I put to my heavenly Father. I pray His glory might be displayed in me and request "What now?" Or as the pastor Helmut Thielicke would say, "To what end?" Yet though our Father promises to hear the cries of His children, He has not promised to exhaustively reveal His mind or plans. We must trust Him—and sometimes in the dark. I am reminded of a story I heard many years ago.

Prior to becoming a professor of philosophy at St. Louis

University, John Kavanaugh traveled to India to work along-side Mother Teresa in Kolkata at the House of the Dying. At one point, he sought the spiritual direction of this slight and suffering saint. He was unsure of his future plans, his calling, and he beseeched her to pray for clarity. She refused.

"Clarity," she said, "is the last thing you are clinging to and must let go of." Instead, she said she would pray for trust. When Kavanaugh expressed his assumption that Mother Teresa always had a clear vision of her calling, she laughed and told him, "I have never had clarity; what I have always had is trust. So I will pray that you trust God."[2] She was, no doubt, familiar with the words of the apostle Paul: "we walk by faith, not by sight" (2 Cor. 5:7).

In whom are we trusting? All is not hidden from us. We do not have exhaustive knowledge, but we have what we need. In the presence of Jesus, by the power of the Holy Spirit, I can know God. I can know the character of my Father. And I can lean into the truth that I am His daughter in whom He delights.

6

Even the darkest night will end and the sun will rise.

—Herbert Kretzmer, in *Les Misérables*[3]

As my dear friend Leslie posted late the evening of the injury, my surgeon bore grim news to family and friends who'd been anxiously waiting and praying for hours at the hospital. He told them breathing tubes had been inserted down my throat, an incision made across my neck, and broken fragments had been removed along with the disc that had been crushing my spinal cord. Donor bone was then used to put my spine back together. Hardware was fused into my spine.

I might eventually come off the ventilator.

Beyond that, hope was discouraged. The surgeon was a realist, and this was a situation that required sobriety and integrity. Paralysis is not for the faint of heart.

And yet, we did hope. In the valley of the night, we strained our eyes in search of some heavenly light. None could discern or understand the story my heavenly Father was writing for me, but we knew there was healing in Jesus. We knew that though doctors are gifted, they are daily met with the realization that their abilities and understanding are limited. We leaned into Jesus, the Son of God, whose body, once broken, was now risen. We knew there was healing in His wings.

7

"What do you fear, lady?" [Aragorn] asked.
"A cage," [Éowyn] said.

—J. R. R. Tolkien, *The Return of the King*

I regained consciousness after surgery late that night; my body was a cage.

I could not breathe.

Nor could I see . . . or move.

My lungs struggled against the tubes in my throat.

My contact lenses had been removed prior to surgery; I could, therefore, only hear voices and see large shadowy masses that I discerned as people. A bleak fear gripped my heart; my eyes became wild and afraid. Unable to communicate that I could not breathe, I heard a female voice. She understood. She implored me to cough and extracted the elongated breathing tube from my throat. My inability to see coupled with my inability to move created a whole new level of terror.

I was completely helpless in my caged body.

8

A scar means, I survived. In a few breaths' time I will speak some sad words to you. But you must hear them the same way we have agreed to see scars now. Sad words are just another beauty. A sad story means, this storyteller is alive. The next thing you know, something fine will happen to her, something marvelous, and then she will turn around and smile.

—Chris Cleave, *Little Bee*

I awoke with a four-inch laceration across the front of my neck covered by a large neck brace and angry pain like I had never in my life experienced. Buzzing, throbbing pain. Burning, fiery pain throughout my body. And an ever intensifying sensation that I was being crushed beneath the weight of an elephant.

In an effort to manage the pain, I was plunged into a sea of round-the-clock drugs. I, who do not even like to take aspirin, felt my mind descend into deep and murky waters. Even so, some events broke powerfully through the muddied haze.

I remember family and friends cramped in my little room, standing at the foot of my bed.

I remember my big brother sleeping in the chair next to me at night so John could be home with the kids.

I remember being dropped on the floor by the nurses attempting to move me to the showers. They were unprepared for the dead weight of my body, and I landed awkwardly and slid halfway under my bed. Panic ensued. A legion of nurses rapidly converged upon my room and, without much finesse, hauled me back into bed. I remember that my brother, livid when he heard what had happened, sent the nurses away.

I remember my friend—the one I stood up for dinner—arriving on the heels of this incident. When she heard what had just happened, she climbed into bed with me, lay beside me, and began to cry. Our tears flowed together as we lamented my body once again colliding with an unforgiving, uninviting surface. After our tears had been spent, she gave me a bath in my bed (she is not only a friend but is also a nurse).

I remember there were visitors, family from afar. But I do not remember our conversations. I remember that I do not ever again want to be on those drugs that made my mind out of control.

I remember deep sadness, fear, acute pain . . . and the nearness of my sweet Savior Jesus.

To know Jesus Christ, dear reader, is to possess a heart of hope—a heart that dares to persist in faith in the midst of the dark night, against the pain and pressures of life because you are not alone, you belong to some*one*. Hope is the continuance, the expression of faith. It's not the same as optimism where one closes her eyes, covers her ears, and thinks positive thoughts. Hope does not double as wishing, the whimsical tossing of pennies into a fountain. Forced or contrived "hope" exposes its inferior underbelly with hope for rain, hope that the cake turns out, that we miss traffic, or "have a good day"; biblical hope is far more concrete.

> Now faith is the assurance of things hoped for, the conviction of things not seen. (Heb. 11:1)

Biblical hope speaks to the believer of assurance and expectation. In my heart, I knew *that* Jesus could heal me, and this would neither tax nor burden His power. I did not, however, know *when* He would heal me. We prayed He would redeem my once strong and agile thirty-four-year-old body so that I could live into these days this side of glory as He intended, with strength and grace.

I found the truth in C. S. Lewis's words, "We are not necessarily doubting that God will do the best for us; we are wondering how painful the best will turn out to be." How much suffering would I have to endure and for how long? When pain is coupled with an undetermined amount of time, without the assurance that relief is coming soon, this is the perilous playground of doubt and despair.

A life of chronic pain lived in a bed with twenty-four-hour care stared me in the face. Did we fear or grieve the possibility that my healing may not occur until I was called home to be with Him?

While this reality lived in our hearts, we kept our eyes open for the miraculous with joyful, confident expectation.

9

"But perhaps you do not understand, I was crippled by an elephant! Crippled by an elephant that came through the roof!"

—Kate DiCamillo, *The Magician's Elephant*

I was not crippled by an elephant. Unlike the elderly woman in DiCamillo's beautifully penned story *The Magician's Elephant*, I wasn't crushed by an elephant that fell out of the sky, through a roof, and into a theater seat at a magic show. That's not my story. Whenever I do tell my story, however, I get the same looks of astonishment, puzzlement, and wonder that I imagine followed this woman's proclamation that she was crushed by an elephant. Like the woman, something, or should I say *someone*, fell from the sky, landing directly on my head.

A week after my surgery, I was transferred to Mary Free Bed, a rehabilitation hospital with a specialized spinal cord injury program. The day I arrived, my room seemed like it had a revolving door. Therapists, doctors, nurses, nursing assistants came to introduce themselves. They all seemed amiable. I don't remember anything they said. But John remembers one conversation acutely. In the hallway outside my room, my physiatrist, a doctor specializing in spinal cord injury and rehabilitation, told John life as he knew it was over, that I was not the same woman he knew a week ago. He told John to get back to pursuing his doctorate, to complete his dissertation, and let the rehab hospital worry about me.

The next morning, the first morning in my new surroundings, I met spunky, diminutive but very pregnant Ashley, affectionately nicknamed "wicked Ashley" by John. She was incredibly capable and fiercely protective of me. My first interaction with my petite but mighty nursing assistant involved a most memorable conversation. She told me she was going to be taking care of me and that meant she had the job of administering an enema and assisting me with a shower. I was mortified by the first proposition; the second duty left me feeling vulnerable, embarrassed yet grateful, as I hadn't had a proper shower in over a week. Talk about fast-tracking the status of our relationship. There was literally nothing between us. Ashley rolled and pushed me from side to side, removing my hospital gown. She then strapped my naked, limp body into a harness and used a crane to transfer me from my bed to a gray plastic chair on wheels. She covered me slightly and drove the chair into the bathroom shower located at the entryway of my room.

After testing the temperature of the water, Ashley pushed

the chair beneath the stream and began to wash my skin, my hair, my nakedness.

Once again, my life felt surreal, as I watched this kind stranger, pregnant as she was, bend over to wash my toes. As I slumped in the gray plastic chair, the water poured over my bare skin.

This is not my life, I silently protested.
Deep breath.
This is some kind of a nightmare.
Only it was not a nightmare. It was painfully, discernibly palpable.

10

"Oh, really," said Roscuro, "this is too extraordinary.
This is too wonderful. I must tell Botticelli that he was
wrong. Suffering is not the answer. Light is the answer."

—Kate DiCamillo, *The Tale of Despereaux*

We were never meant to die. That wasn't the plan. Contrary to the popular notion that death is simply a part of life, death is a contradiction of life—contrary to who we are and who God is. We were made to live in fellowship with the triune God of life. Yet with sin came death. With sin came suffering.

I will not try to explain suffering. Evil and suffering make no sense. Why do children die . . . or people lose their minds? Why are some lives lived with chronic pain . . . loneliness . . . or under the tyranny of violence? Why do atrocities happen every minute of every day? Why does suffering find its way into the homes of every neighbor down the street . . . and to every man, woman, and child across the globe? My knee-jerk response is to answer *because of sin*. But why? *Because of the fall . . . Because of Satan . . .*

But again, *why*?

At some point, we must admit that though we can recognize it, we cannot understand, we cannot explain away evil. The sheer madness and incongruity of sin is expressed in the writings of Karl Barth:

> Sin has no basis. It has, therefore, no possibility—we cannot escape this difficult formula—except that of the absolutely impossible. . . . Sin is that which is absurd, man's absurd choice and decision for that which is not. [4]

Put simply, sin makes no sense. To explain and come to an understanding of sin is to justify it, to reconcile what can never be reconciled. Sin is illogical, irrational, impossible, absurd by creational categories. It is humanity unhinged, humankind decisively breaking from the One who gave them life, the One who has only ever sought to bless His created with every good gift. And we are deep in it. The darkness, the sadness, and wickedness is felt from without *and* within.

When I was six months pregnant with our first child, I arrived at the hospital for a routine monthly checkup. I knew the appointment was going to take a bit longer than usual as I was having the glucose tolerance test for gestational

diabetes, so John didn't join me. I drank the sugary substance then waited, as required, for an hour. I recall that
the friendly nurse, Angela, summoned me after the hour,
escorted me to a room, and began the follow-up testing.

Soon the doctor was in the room listening to the baby's
heart rate. *Strange*, I thought. *She doesn't usually listen to
the heartbeat.* I soon learned the reason for her presence;
my astute nurse had discovered a tachycardia—extreme
rapidity in William's heart rate. Later ultrasounds would
reveal that his upper chambers were beating 450 beats per
minute, while the ventricles, trying hard to keep up, were
racing at 225 beats a minute. A normal heart rate for a baby
is between 120 and 180 beats per minute.

I still have the diagram of our son's preborn heart
sketched by one of my bold, good-humored doctors. Dr.
Patton explained what was happening—William's thumb-
sized heart was being stimulated with rapid electrical signals
causing the upper chambers to beat at an accelerated rate;
the lower chambers could not match the lightning-fast
cadence, which was causing fluid to pool around his heart,
belly, and lungs. But though our perinatologist told us he
could explain *what* was happening, this world-class special-
ist couldn't begin to explain *why* it was happening.

The answers to many "why" questions are unreachable
and beyond our comprehension. Perhaps when we are at
the end of the story, we'll know more—as is often the case

with stories. Sometimes, I admit, I get bogged down in the suffering.

My heart, even when I was young, was gripped by bitter tales of sorrow. When I began to study art as a teenager, I quickly came to love Van Gogh. The loneliness he wrote about in his letters to his brother rapped on and resounded in my heart. I was captured by the children at the day-care center where I worked who came from broken, divorced families. I was drawn to suffering; I let it make a home in my heart.

But within the din of sorrow rings more clearly the truth discovered by Kate DiCamillo's character Roscuro: *Suffering is not the answer. Light is the answer.* Or as explained beautifully by the apostle Peter:

> But you are a chosen race, a royal priesthood, a holy nation, a people for his own possession, that you may proclaim the excellencies of him who called you out of darkness into his marvelous light. Once you were not a people, but now you are God's people; once you had not received mercy, but now you have received mercy. (1 Peter 2:9–10)

We belong in the light. But we live in the shadow, the shadow of brokenness, of despair, of sickness and sin. We do not, however, live alone in this shadow. We are joined to the triune God who suffers with us. The Enemy whispers, *You are alone. You are not seen, nor are you loved.* The blood and wounds of Jesus, however, say otherwise. To this end, theologian Tom Torrance expounds:

> God does not offer us any explanation for evil, but deals decisively and finally with it by entering himself into its abysmal chasm separating us from him and bridging it through the atoning life and death of his incarnate Son. At the same time the fact that God himself had to make atonement in order to save us, reveals the bottomless nature of the discontinuity between man and God which nothing else and no one else could bridge.[5]

When we tore ourselves from the arms of the Father, we created a wake of sorrow and suffering, of chaos and confusion, a titanic chasm between us and God. No bridge, save Jesus, is capable of restoring and reuniting us with the Father. At times it may feel as if we're groping through the darkness. But rest assured, dear reader, we are never alone. And when we cling to Jesus, when we grab hold of Him when life is dark and silent, we are brought into the light, even if at first it seems to only be a small flicker of light.

It is perhaps during these dark times that we come to know our Jesus. In the bleak, black night, we taste the sorrow felt by Him in the dark garden of Gethsemane. By our wounds and pain we touch the broken body of Jesus, and feel the weight of the cross on His back. Our suffering makes way for us to enter into His passion. Any longing we suffer, He has suffered first.

When our hearts break over lives lost to addiction, we are united in His sorrow.

When we grieve the violence waged against children, we are picking up His cross.

When we cry over souls far from God, now we begin to conceive the heart of our triune God. Flannery O'Connor once said, "You will have found Christ when you are concerned with other people's suffering and not your own."

When our hearts suffer with and for others, we image Jesus. We participate in the suffering of Jesus just as He enters in and joins us in ours. But He has not come merely to walk alongside us extending compassion and empathy, as lovely and significant as this is. He enters into the very chaos of our lives, joining Himself to us with an aim to overcome; He comes not to exalt but to dispel the darkness.

11

Real courage is when you know you're licked before you begin, but you begin anyway and see it through no matter what.

—Harper Lee, *To Kill a Mockingbird*

Shortly after I arrived at the rehabilitation hospital, Gwyneth witnessed me being transferred from my hospital bed into my power wheelchair.

A nursing assistant rolled me to one side, placed some material under me, rolled me to the other side, and adjusted the material some more. She pressed a button, elevating the bed into an upright position. The cloth was then clipped to a crane mechanism that lowered from the ceiling. With the switch of a remote control device, I was suspended high in the air above my bed. My body was limp; my legs dangled.

The nurse told my daughter, "Look, your mom is flying." Gwyneth, ever perceptive and not amused, curtly replied, "No, she's not."

Flying? Dear God, I couldn't even sit up in bed by my own strength. I couldn't wipe the tears from my little girl's face. I couldn't brush her tangled mess of hair. No, I was certainly not flying.

Life as our family knew it seemed to be over. Perhaps William said it best. Through tears he told his dad that when that boy jumped on Mom, he jumped on our entire family. Gone were the days of running and laughing, of piggyback rides and dancing. Ours was a family that loved to dance; we'd crank the radio after dinner and dance while we cleared the plates and tidied the kitchen. Sometimes we'd just abandon the kitchen work altogether so we could spin each other around the room. I used to joke that I was born in the wrong time period. I would have loved the Roaring Twenties' dance club craze or the fifties when everyone seemed to break into spontaneous, though well-choreographed, song and dance.

On Thursdays, I would jog to a nearby gym to participate in my favorite high-spirited fitness class, Zumba. I also ran a few times a week (which is not nearly as diverting, entertaining, or amusing as Zumba), and I was looking forward to adding bike rides to our family outings; we were always seeking and devising ways to be outside.

Before the accident, I worked from home, writing for a Christian ministry. And I traveled one to two times a month, helping my employer at conferences. One weekend when I was away, a surprise was brewing. "I have something to show you," Gwyneth delightedly chirped as John and the kids met me at the airport. When we arrived home, she took me to the parking lot next to our house, climbed on her bike—minus the training wheels—and sped away like a pro. I jumped, clapped, and watched as my four-year-old swerved and pedaled and relished this moment—this grand rite of passage.

A few weeks later my little tribe of three, looking as if they'd been cheating at poker, sported sly mischievous grins. On Mother's Day, I walked into the kitchen and found a light-blue bike. I was stunned (and slightly horrified) at the extravagant gift. We were living on my small salary until John finished his dissertation, and he and I rarely purchased gifts for each other. But I could not deny the giddy, ennobled hearts of William and Gwyneth. They were thrilled at the thought of trailblazing new territory together across western Michigan.

Nineteen days later, dust and cobwebs began to collect on our cycling dreams.

I had, like virtually all moms, an abundant, active life. A life teeming with movement. More often than not, I bounded two steps at a time up our flight of stairs. I jogged to and from our vehicle. I skillfully darted and weaved through airports.

Now I was reduced to lying in bed wondering if I would ever again be able to enfold my flesh and blood in my arms, to feel their warmth against my skin. Outside the rehab hospital, lavender lilacs were in bloom; their intoxicating fragrance could be caught in the breeze. Outside, busy lives buzzed—driving, laughing, working, joining in spring sports, basking in the warmth of the sun.

Within the doors of Mary Free Bed, however, life seemed to halt, frozen in an atmosphere stagnant with despair and disinfectant. Though the outside world kept spinning, it spun apart from those of us inside. We were defective twirling tops lying uselessly on our sides waiting to be animated, desperate to play and be embodied in the rhythm of life once again.

My friends posted Bible verses in my room. I can still picture the blue ink printed on white paper with royal blue construction paper background.

Be strong and courageous. Do not be afraid;
do not be discouraged, for the LORD your God
will be with you wherever you go.
Joshua 1:9 [NIV]

I can do all things through him who strengthens me.
Philippians 4:13

But he said to me, "My grace is sufficient for you,
for my power is made perfect in weakness."
2 Corinthians 12:9 [NIV]

But the Lord stood at my side and gave me
strength, so that through me the
message might be fully proclaimed.
2 Timothy 4:17 [NIV]

Every time I sat in bed, these verses instructed, strengthened, and put courage into my heart. Not because the words themselves possessed some kind of magic, but because by the power of the Holy Spirit they brought me near to my heavenly Father and His glorious Son, Jesus Christ.

When fear attempted to put its arm around me like a familiar friend, I was reminded that I was not alone.

When doubts buffeted my soul, I was reassured of my heavenly Father's love for me.

When sorrow weighed like an anchor upon my heart, I was comforted by Jesus, the One who'd known tears and suffering, the One who now entered my pain and anguish.

In the midst of this seemingly hopeless situation, the Grand Rapids community prayed—bold prayers, prayers for a healing, a miracle—and we continued to trust in the wisdom and power of our triune God.

My daughter asked her daddy if it was okay to pray that Mom would walk again. The doctors had already addressed this concern: *No, she will not walk again. She may make some progress; but be assured, she is going to need long-term care.*

We were tempted to stonewall ourselves from disappointment, to insulate and inoculate ourselves in disbelief and follow the way of Edward the rabbit, a character from one of John's favorite Kate DiCamillo stories, *The Miraculous Journey of Edward Tulane*. Edward "prided himself on not hoping, on not allowing his heart to lift inside of him. He prided himself on keeping his heart silent, immobile, closed tight."[6]

But now was not the time to latch the shutters over our hearts. Instead we dared to throw them open, to lay them bare, weak and vulnerable as they were.

John told his fragile girl, "Yes, pray that Mom will walk again."

PART TWO

the journey

12

Crying is all right in its way while it lasts. But you have to stop sooner or later, and then you still have to decide what to do.

—C. S. Lewis, *The Silver Chair*

And so the journey began.

Each morning a pleasant young man named Max woke me up around five o'clock to take my blood pressure. This was followed by a shot in the belly, given by the attending nurse. Then meds. Catheterization. Then a trip to the shower where a stranger, often a kind stranger, would begin the humiliating and always unsuccessful process of administering an enema, followed by the shampooing of my hair and washing of my body. I would then be dried and pushed back to my bed. The slow, laborious process of dressing me followed. Another stranger would brush my teeth and comb my hair.

Oftentimes breakfast would be sitting on a tray over my bed. And I would sit and wait until someone would open the packages and feed me. Many of the "strangers" treated me with such dignity and gentleness I still want to cry when I think about it. I came to know much of the hospital staff during my lengthy stay. They became friends, entering my valley of pain, shame, loss, and grief.

The downbeat of my day went something like this with mornings and afternoons a full onslaught of therapy.

Occupational therapy: My occupational therapist was also an Ashley, but of a more angelic type. Whereas my nursing assistant was like a force of nature, this Ashley was like a gentle breeze. The young, golden-haired therapist spoke calmly and softly. She greeted me almost every morning in my room. She slowly dressed me: compression hosiery to prevent blood clots, braces to support my collapsing wrists, Depends, shorts, T-shirt, socks, tennis shoes. Each morning she arrived calm and pleasant, and helped me dress and eat. Her role was to teach me how to perform daily tasks necessary for living. Brush teeth, brush hair, hold a fork, get food on the fork, get the fork to my mouth, open items, anything and everything having to do with my hands.

In addition to seeing Ashley every morning in my room, I met with her in the large therapy room on the first floor of the hospital twice a day, late morning and early afternoon. There, she tested my hand strength. "Squeeze this." Hmm, at first I couldn't even hold it, so she helped me. "Now, squeeze." Nothing. After every test, she wrote, "Absent." We had our work cut out for us.

I did have some mobility in my arms. But that was often

suspect. An assistant named Jen was assigned to strengthen my upper body. Ashley homed in on my hands. She had the most challenging assignment of anyone. She was painfully patient and flawlessly focused. What a contrast to me. Prior to my injury, I thrived on working in fast-forward. I was a strategic driver, aware of the fastest lanes and quickest routes. I grocery shopped with speed and precision; when I walked, I did so with purpose. Ashley's patient pace humbled me.

Eventually, she timed me at picking up little pegs and placing them in holes. This was an activity we practiced repeatedly over the next year. I hated it. Ashley was a dear. She was never bored nor did she give the impression that *This is taking forever!* My stomach churned, my frustration mounted, and I could not help but feel that I was wasting this precious young woman's time.

Respiratory therapy: The injury had literally knocked the breath out of me. Additionally, my surgeon had made his incision at the front of my neck. Therefore, my vocal cords had to be exposed and adjusted in order to reach my spine. In respiratory therapy, we worked on getting my lungs and voice back to full capacity, and we focused on my brain. I did not lose consciousness upon impact and, therefore, did not seem to have a brain injury. And yet my brain was sometimes in a fog. My mental capacities lacked sharpness and clarity.

Physical therapy: Tracy and an intern named Erin were

charged with the challenge of helping me regain muscle functionality and increased mobility. They began by testing my strength, which hardly registered. But not all hope was lost. I did have some mobility; it began with my left foot. I could move it ever so slightly, and I did so every chance I could. This little piece of normal, even if the doctors said not to get too excited, was thrilling.

My right side was weaker than my left, which wasn't saying much at the start, but as I progressed, the contrast was more noticeable. My physician's assistant, Lindsay, did strengthening exercises with my unresponsive, heavy-laden legs every day. In time, I was strapped into a machine that did the walking for me. It lifted my legs in an effort to establish muscle memory, to retrain my brain.

Pool therapy: A crane was again employed to lift me out of my power wheelchair and into a pool. The buoyancy of the water encouraged my brain and muscles. What was impossible on dry land seemed plausible in the pool. Small steps, always with a therapist at my side.

One day I met a man in the pool who'd tripped over a trailer hitch and broken his neck. He was walking in the pool with his assistant, sometimes as far as twenty feet. He had been at Mary Free Bed for almost a year. He spoke words of encouragement—maybe I too would someday be walking like he was.

Therapy, therapy, and more therapy: As part of my rehabilitation, I was assigned to see a psychiatrist. The first time I met the doctor, she asked me to tell her what happened. As I recounted the events of my injury, I sobbed like a baby. And as you can imagine, for someone who was unable to employ the use of a Kleenex, I was a mess of tears and snot. She listened. She told me I was grieving and not depressed. I knew that, but I was glad to hear her say it.

Recreational therapy: I was also enlisted for recreational therapy, which most closely resembled occupational therapy. Here I would focus on getting back to life—a broken life. Life in a wheelchair. How to navigate getting on an airplane in a power wheelchair. How to start playing games again. One day a young intern rattled off the names of several games and asked what games I liked to play prior to my injury. Battleship? She set up the two boards. More little pegs? I wanted to cry. How about cards? I grew up in a card-playing family. I was familiar with poker, euchre, solitaire. Shuffling cards now was obviously out of the question. Maybe if she just put them in my hand for me. No again. I lacked the feeling or coordination to hold or maneuver any of my digits.

All my therapy was supervised by a physiatrist—a doctor who specializes in physical medicine and rehabilitation—whom I saw every day in my hospital room.

In the late afternoons, I would power my wheelchair back to the third floor; my room was the first door on the left after the nurses' station. Sometimes I had the space to myself, which served my somewhat introverted personality well. But I was never alone for long. I needed help getting into my bed. I needed pain medication. I needed someone to catheterize me. Family came. I was always grateful to have a family member feed me (even my kids who did not have great aim).

In order to create some "normalcy" in our lives, we established a family dinnertime. One of my friends set up a meal calendar. Families and staff from William's school, friends, and brothers and sisters in Jesus Christ, many from our home church, Church of the Servant, delivered warm dinners and sweet desserts to the hospital. Word traveled fast in the close Dutch community of Grand Rapids. Even Will and Gwen's pediatrician brought us meals. Much of the food was gifts from the hands of strangers. The kids delighted in sharing with the nurses what seemed like a never-ending stream of cupcakes, cookies, cake, and confections. We asked visitors to come after 6:15 p.m. so we could have this time together as a family.

Our seven- and four-year-old became well acquainted with trauma. Brain injury patients with a vacant look in their eyes, shaved heads, or black exposed stitches passed them in the hallways. Stroke patients, easily identified as the only patients on their feet, shuffled along in the large therapy room. Injured or sick children were in a different wing of the hospital and mostly had therapy in their rooms, but sometimes we'd see a little one wearing a protective helmet or in a wheelchair.

One family with whom we became friends had a daughter who'd suffered severe complications during a seemingly routine tonsillectomy. The red-haired teenager had suffered brain damage and was blind. Our kids befriended a gang of motorcyclists who often came to visit their friend who'd taken a spill on his Harley-Davidson. In addition to gaining some tattooed mates, Will and Gwen were embraced by the hospital staff. Soon, my kids knew their way around the hospital. And one bright spot was a cafeteria with a freezer full of ice cream treats. If you ask my kids about what they remember about the hospital, this is often one of their first recollections.

No doubt they were affected by the myriad of once strong people who were now broken in body and some in spirit; but God, in His mercy, impressed upon William's and Gwyneth's young minds ice cream novelties, Animal Planet (we did not have cable, so this was a special treat at the hospital), and memorable friends.

In the evenings, John would take William and Gwyneth home to tuck them in for the night. Then he would often leave the kids with family visiting from out of town and hurry back to me. This was treasured time.

Twelve days after my injury, John posted on my Care Page:

As you can imagine, I'm usually at Mary Free Bed several times daily. Yet it's my after-hours visits with Kate that are far and away the sweetest, because it's during these visits that we're most able to be really present with one another. Every one of them is marked by laughter and tears—we grieve, but are neither discouraged nor depressed. And every one of them is marked by a mounting sense of hope and gratitude—a sense that God is not only near, but that He is doing something mighty and altogether lovely in our midst.

What is more, I want you to know that beyond Kate's physical progress, she is thriving. She is terrifically determined, and she seems to grow daily in faith, hope, love, and joy. As I spend time with her, I come away with the deep sense that Kate is becoming a trophy of God's grace in Jesus Christ. To my delight, and admittedly, my surprise, I find that Kate has become even more beautiful to me, and that I am even more in love with her than I was before the accident.

Speaking of the support of loved ones, I want you all to know that the messages you send Kate on her Care Page mean more to her than I could express. She eagerly awaits having them read to her every single day, and their effect on her is quite dramatic. Thank you so very much for your kindness!! I'll write more as I'm able.

The peace of Christ to you all,
John

After laughing and crying together each night, John would brush my teeth, kiss my head, and tell me, "Tomorrow, I want you to get a little bit better."

In the dark, I'd lie in bed. Every few hours a nursing assistant would interrupt my slumber to shift the position of my body in order to prevent pressure sores. Pillows were stuffed all around me. One of my favorite nighttime caregivers was a sweet, sensitive, Christian woman. She moved my body with extreme care and gentleness; she flipped the pillow beneath my head for a cool sensation on my neck. She catheterized me. She prayed for me. And she left a book for John filled with Scripture verses. Before each of the assistants left, they placed an oversized red plastic button a few inches away from my hand. If I needed help, I could knock it with the back or side of my hand, which would then send a signal to the nurses' station.

At five o'clock the next morning, the cycle repeated.

13

Real miracles bother people, like strange sudden pains unknown in medical literature. It's true: They rebut every rule all we good citizens take comfort in. Lazarus obeying orders and climbing up out of the grave—now there's a miracle, and you can bet it upset a lot of folks who were standing around at the time. When a person dies, the earth is generally unwilling to cough him back up. A miracle contradicts the will of earth.

—Leif Enger, *Peace Like a River*

Movement does not equal miracle. I was able to compel my left foot to move—ever so slightly and with a colossal amount of effort. This, the doctors were clear to point out, was not a miracle. Sometimes, some patients with spinal cord injuries experience a small amount of functioning in their limbs.

Functioning isn't quite the right word. The motion is often crude. Spastic. Awkward. At times the movement is not even deliberate—muscles jerking out of control.

Nothing very sturdy on which to hang your hopes. Indeed, it would be foolish to place too much hope here.

I've mentioned that I was outfitted with a power wheelchair. This heavily mechanized carrier had a simple joystick that even a child could instantly master, as did my children. But even in its simplicity, the device was too challenging and ambitious for me—at first. In my early rehabilitation days, a nurse or family member would drive the chair for me. One day, a staff member walked alongside me and directed my chair to a level of the hospital where I had been assigned recreational therapy. She left me in a room, and I waited— what else could I do?—for the therapist.

This therapist arrived bright and happy, manipulating her own wheelchair. She had a lower-level spinal cord injury resulting in little to no movement below the waist, but she had full ability in her upper extremities. She explained that we were going to work on maneuvering my wheelchair.

"Today," she said, "we're going to concentrate on mastering life in a wheelchair; for example, how to get on and off the airplane using your power chair." She knew I had traveled for work prior to my injury, and evidently thought this would be a most beneficial use of our time. I didn't quite understand.

"I don't even know if I'm going to need a wheelchair," I hesitantly, shyly confessed. "I think I might just walk on and off that plane."

She looked at me with troubled eyes. She even seemed a

little embarrassed for me. *Poor girl,* her eyes seemed to say. *She's still stuck in the very first stage of the Kübler-Ross model of grief: DENIAL.*

I felt a heat climbing in my cheeks and was transported to the bus stop of my early elementary years. One day while waiting with my three older siblings for the bus to collect and take us to school, an older kid with a condescending laugh asked me if I believed in Santa Claus. "No," I uttered a little too forcibly. "Of course not," I scoffed stormily. I turned my face away, burning with self-consciousness, the shame of my gullibility. *I've been such a fool.* Oh, how I hated to play the part of the fool. To be sure, no one revels in playing the fool, but when you're the youngest of four, this is a particularly tender spot. Here I was, years later, with another Santa Claus moment. A voice in my head said, *Kate, you're behaving like a child. When are you going to grow up? You'd need a miracle to walk onto a plane. And a miracle is the stuff of legends and fairy tales.*

Or is it? Here with my therapist I felt once again like a joke, the wide-eyed child at the bus stop. I was in a delicate predicament. I could either drop the part of the fool, smother this childish belief, and bravely face my future.

Or I could give hope room to breathe.

I found myself uttering again and again, day after day, the prayer of the father in the gospel of Mark: "I believe; help my unbelief!" (9:24). I took my place alongside the troubled, doubting, sometimes accusing people in Scripture. I'm no hero. I found solace knowing that the same unbreakable bond shared between the Father, Son, and Holy Spirit held me. Just as the members of the Trinity could never be severed from one another, my union with Jesus Christ assured that no one or nothing—not even my own frail heart—could separate me from the life and love of the triune God. I petitioned Him for what I could not myself do.

I believe, Lord; help my unbelief.

14

Everyone has a moment in history which belongs particularly to him. It is the moment when his emotions achieve their most powerful sway over him, and afterward when you say to this person "the world today" or "life" or "reality" he will assume that you mean this moment, even if it is fifty years past. The world, through his unleashed emotions, imprinted itself upon him, and he carries the stamp of that passing moment forever.

—John Knowles, *A Separate Peace*

In an instant, all of life can change. Sometimes it's because of a decision we've made. At times it's thrust upon us by the choice of another. And other times it's just the result of living in this broken world.

May 29, 2009 was an indelible mark, a branding if you will, on our family history. Seared on our hearts was a radiant Friday in May, a playground outside an elementary school, a fall. From this day forward, we carried the stamp of that passing moment that subtly began to categorize and dominate our lives.

"Before" or "after" May 29, 2009? I see a photograph. "When was this taken?" "Oh, this was *before* I got hurt." Or, "I remember that. That was *after* the injury." All pictures, birthdays, school grades, celebrations, trips, significant and not so significant events are filtered quite unintentionally by the momentous May 29th date and then sorted and placed into one of two main file cabinets in our brains, "before" or "after."

Music has a particular way of transporting us in time. Paul Simon reminds me of the days when we'd dance as we cleared the dinner dishes—*before* the injury. That whimsical tradition ended the day I fell. Now I hear the Beatles' song "Here Comes the Sun" and think, *Prior to my injury, this was the tune that got my heart pumping and sneakers pounding the pavement each time I embarked on a run.* Other songs cause me to reminisce; I loved to run to this song. Now, when I see joggers advancing rapidly along the sidewalk, I muse, *That was me pre-injury.*

The artist Mat Kearney released a song titled "Closer to Love" that became popular around the time of my release from the hospital. This tune has a distinct way of ferrying me back to Grand Rapids. It begins with the story of a girl who gets a devastating phone call—a call with news that levels her.

For almost an entire year, we kept my message on our answering machine from May 29th imploring John to pick up the phone. We wouldn't listen to it—instead we'd hit the fast-forward button as soon as it began to play. Yet we couldn't bring ourselves to erase that life-changing moment captured in that simple machine when all of life seemed to split apart. Kearney's song[7] continues much like a modern day psalm of lament. "Cryin' out now . . . Prayin' Lord come through . . ."

I felt as if we were living in this song. I was indeed brought low before Him, asking, *Lord, please come through*. I crumpled under the truth that I was weary of trying to be strong. Oh, how tired I had become. Tired in my bones. Both John and I were felled by a fatigue that would not be alleviated with a good nap or full night of rest. This exhaustion had left a mark, a bruise still present today, purple and tender. I can sometimes listen to Kearney's lyrics now and stem the tide of tears, but I cannot hear them without thinking about those dark and beautiful days suffered in the valley.

The archiving of time via May 29th doesn't necessarily highlight a loss. It's simply a historical data point. We moved one year after the injury. We took that trip two years before I got hurt. John finished his doctorate three years after Kate's fall. We got the computer I'm currently typing on a few weeks after May 29th—a gift from my oldest brother who couldn't bear our lackadaisical, turtle-esque laptop.

When the specific day—the anniversary—pops up on our calendar, I am a myriad of emotions. Do we "celebrate"? Sometimes I hear people reminisce about tragedy in their lives. They say, "I would go through it all over again in a heartbeat." I think they're saying that they came out of the hardship so changed it was all worth it. I am not denying that. Yet, I cannot bring myself to share the "I would do it all over again" sentiment. I do not desire to relive that death.

Some years on May 29th I pray in the little chapel at our church. I thank God for His miraculous work, and I petition my heavenly Father to redeem the pain and suffering. I give thanks, as I have not forgotten what it feels like to need feeding, bathroom, and showering assistance. I have not buried the memories of my children's sorrow. I praise. I grieve.

Most people have forgotten that May 29th is the day of my injury. That's okay. It's not their moment in history. Others have their own moments, their own literal or proverbial phone call that brought them to their knees. The day someone they loved died. The day the doctor said, "cancer." The moment that car came crashing out of nowhere. These days and moments belong to the sufferer.

There are a few friends and family members, of course, who do still remember. Several people entered into my suffering in such a way that it became their pain and sorrow as well. I found a book with a card on my doorstop six years to the day after my injury from my dear friend who traveled from Chicago to Grand Rapids the day after I fell. I know that God remembers. Yet my friend's gift is a tangible truth from God. "Yes, Kate, I see you."

Does time indeed *heal all wounds*? Contrary to the old adage, time is not a restoring agent. Jesus alone is healer. If repair takes place in the darkness apart from Him, devoid of His warmth and light, our hearts and minds mend crookedly and become misshapen. The break, not set properly, leads to a distorted putting back together of oneself. The broken, bitter, and betrayed soul becomes like a wounded animal that hides away or snarls and bears his teeth whenever someone or something comes near.

Time races and taunts . . . sometimes it seems to stand still . . . but it does not heal. The poem *As I Walked Out One Evening*[8] by W. H. Auden rings true:

> But all the clocks in the city
> Began to whirr and chime:
> "O let not Time deceive you,
> You cannot conquer Time."

May 29, 2009 is a moment in history belonging to our family—the breaking of our family. But, of course, there is another moment in history, an indelible stamp, far more pressing and powerful on our lives. God sought to put us back together—via the incarnation—centuries *before* our shattering. Each December we celebrate and claim for our own Jesus Christ, who entered time and willingly subjected Himself to the lessons of crawling, walking, and holding a spoon. He suffered body, mind, and soul, so that, being bound to Him, we might be healed: body, mind, and soul. Then, in what must have seemed like a sudden crack in time, the life of the young, strong thirty-three-year-old Jesus slowly drained as His beaten body hung on a cross.

But was time the victor? Jesus is both the creator and

conqueror—the maker and redeemer of time. As the Son of God, He is not constrained by time. He is eternal and has no beginning. He has known us and His plans for us long before we found ourselves living this mere breath of life that is like a passing shadow.

> For you formed my inward parts; you knitted me together in my mother's womb. (Ps. 139:13)

> Blessed be the God and Father of our Lord Jesus Christ, who has blessed us in Christ with every spiritual blessing in the heavenly places, even as he chose us in him before the foundation of the world, that we should be holy and blameless before him. In love he predestined us for adoption as sons through Jesus Christ, according to the purpose of his will, to the praise of his glorious grace, with which he has blessed us in the Beloved. (Eph. 1:3–6)

Life changed for all of us—John, William, Gwyneth, and me—on the last Friday of May 2009. Yet our lives were already hidden in Jesus Christ. Nothing and no one could pluck us from His hand, nothing and no one could keep us from His almighty love. Someday, when time runs its course and death does indeed come, our lives will continue. Those united with Jesus in His life, death, and resurrection will be called home, will be reunited with the One who loves them and has sacrificed everything for them.

15

It is a fair, even-handed, noble adjustment of things, that while
there is infection in disease and sorrow, there is nothing in the
world so irresistibly contagious as laughter and good-humour.

—Charles Dickens, *A Christmas Carol*

Thinking of You, Mrs. Clark . . . by Mr. Wright's Class was the title of the light-purple spiral-bound book—a gift from my favorite first graders. William leaned into my hospital bed and proudly, slowly, flipped through the laminated pages for me. At the top of each page was a photograph of the student smiling or looking mischievous and below each picture was a personal message in bold print, often with creative spelling and punctuation. Here are a few that brought light and laughter to my day.

> Dear Mrs. Clark, I love you sow much. I wud
> like too visit You and I hope You fil beter.
> Mrs. Mia

Dear Mrs. Clark, I hope you git out from the hospital
and feel beter you are the Best too and read.
love Ali

Dear Mrs. Clarck, I whish you ...... better luck thrue the year.
I hope you feel better soon.
Love, Kaelyn

Dear Mrs. Clark, yuo are the bast redr in the wrld.
Sumtims i mit visit you I hop you fel batr
frum Michael

Dear Mis. Clark, I hope you feel better son. I am sore.
You are a gud techer. I hope you go to Kentucky.
Love, Amea

Dear Mrs. Clark, I hope you feel Beter you are fun and sile
love Keith

Dear Mommy, I love you and hope you can get out of the
hospital soon. I want you to know that I am praying for you.
I wish you could go to Kentucky with us. I am so sorry
you can't go. I am excited to reteach you to walk!
Love, William

Dear Mrs. Clarck, I fel sare for you. I hope that you fel beter.
Joshua

Dear Mrs. Clark, I hope you feel better soon. You are so loving. When my play was over I saw Mr. Bartells.
Sincerely, Sydnie

Dear Mrs. Clark, I hope you feel Better soon. I've had that happend to me before. I know how it feels.
Sincerely, Connor

16

There is a stubbornness about me that never can bear
to be frightened at the will of others. My courage
always rises at every attempt to intimidate me.

—Jane Austen, *Pride and Prejudice*

My dad and mom had four children in five years, two
boys followed by two girls. As I've said, I am the
youngest of the brood.

Unlike the follow-the-leader, happy-go-lucky personalities that some children down the family line possess, I
was more like the runt of the litter ready to scrap. Don't get
me wrong—I wasn't throwing punches in the schoolyard
(actually, I was an easy student who took my education
perhaps a little too seriously). Yet I wasn't one to wilt in the
face of adversity; I was far more likely to plant my feet and
fortify. This on-alert, ready-to-fight disposition has been a
bit of both a blessing and a curse.

Beneath the Scripture verses in my hospital room hung

a metalwork sign with the bold challenge, "Be not afraid,"
a gift from the artist Carol Roeda. The black metal bored
through me; it seemed like a test, and I was not sure I could
pass. When I looked at it, which was often as it was directly
across from my bed, my heart faltered. Instead of a blessing,
it seemed like a taunt, a reproach. I could command my
heart not to fear with the same power I possess to direct the
sun not to rise and with about the same success. *Lord, I am
paralyzed. Literally.*

I chaffed against the instructions to be not afraid. In days
past, when my little ones told me, "I feel sad" or "I'm scared"
I tried not to react with the words, "Don't." "*Don't* be sad" or
"*Don't* be afraid." What a foolish and false friend I would be
if I instructed my children to tamp down seemingly negative
emotions or to deny what was unpleasant, harsh, or hard.
Instead, I endeavored to speak honestly, to empathize with
their pain, to breathe truth into their hearts: "I am sorry you
feel sad. I know how it hurts when others say mean things
about you. But you are loved, dear one. And you have a Savior who knows what it feels like to be misrepresented, who's
acquainted with the backbiting of 'friends.' I know you feel
lonely, but, even so, most assuredly, you are not alone."

Over the years, I've felt liberated by the raw, forthright
pleas and cries of the psalmists.

> Be gracious to me, O LORD, for I am languishing;
>   heal me, O LORD, for my bones are troubled.

My soul also is greatly troubled.
  But you, O LORD—how long? (Ps. 6:2–3)

When my soul was embittered,
  when I was pricked in heart,
I was brutish and ignorant;
  I was like a beast toward you. (Ps. 73:21–22)

My flesh and my heart may fail,
    but God is the strength of my heart and my portion forever. (Ps. 73:26)

Hear my voice, O God, in my complaint;
  preserve my life from dread of the enemy.
Hide me from the secret plots of the wicked,
  from the throng of evildoers,
who whet their tongues like swords,
  who aim bitter words like arrows. (Ps. 64:1–3)

Incline your ear, O LORD, and answer me,
  for I am poor and needy. . . .
Gladden the soul of your servant,
  for to you, O Lord, do I lift up my soul. (Ps. 86:1, 4)

I am poor and needy. I doubt. And sometimes, I am afraid. For are there not things that harass and terrify our hearts? Are there not hardships that bring us to our knees? News stories that make us want to scream or cry or vomit?
  When my children were smaller in frame and terrors

came to them in the night, I would sit on their bed and sing the words of a song that brought my heart comfort. Jack Noble White's "First Song of Isaiah"[9] speaks of trusting in God who saves; to not be afraid, for it is He who is our stronghold and defense.

The context here is crucial. When Scripture speaks of not being afraid, it is always cloaked in the presence of the Lord. Be not afraid, not because the situation isn't terrifying, but because you're not alone. You have a Good Shepherd who hides you beneath His wing. When you are weak and cannot defend yourself, He is your stronghold and defense. He sees and hears the desperation of your soul. He is gracious to those who are languishing.

Courage, dear reader, for He is near. Near in our sorrow. Joined to us in our panic. Rescuing us from our nightmares. He draws us into Himself that He might be the mender of our mangled bodies, the restorer of our tattered souls, and the healer of our fragmented, frustrated minds.

17

*What's cool about really little kids is that they don't
say stuff to try to hurt your feelings, even though
sometimes they do say stuff that hurts your feelings.
But they don't actually know what they're saying.*

—R. J. Palacio, *Wonder*

One weekend I was driving my power wheelchair through the corridors of the hospital on my way to therapy when a young woman stopped, looked down at me, and with a smile asked, "Are you a quadriplegic?"

I was bewildered and slightly shaken. It was the first time I had heard someone refer to me by this label. I don't remember what I said or if I even said anything. I continued maneuvering my mechanized chair to therapy and told the therapist working that weekend about my strange encounter in the hallway. She said I did indeed have quadriplegia.

What? My befuddled brain silently quarreled, *This therapist doesn't even know me. She's just weekend help filling in for the "real" therapists.*

On Monday, I posed the question to Ashley. In her sweet, sympathetic way, she imparted the news to me again. "Did no one talk to you about this yet, Kate?"

Quadriplegia, also known as tetraplegia, is my diagnosis. *Quad* comes from Latin, four, whereas *tetra* is from the Greek. Since *plegia* is Greek, many people in the medical profession have switched to using the Greek-Greek word *tetraplegia* instead of the Latin-Greek combination of *quadriplegia* that is more familiar to the layperson. What is important for our present purposes is that both quadriplegia and tetraplegia mean paralysis of the four limbs: arms and legs.

Prior to my injury, I had always thought quadriplegia was total paralysis from the neck down. This indeed does describe one type of quadriplegia. Incomplete quadriplegia, however, results when some sensation or movement is evident below the point of injury. I was diagnosed with the latter, yet the menacing term *quadriplegia* had not been uttered in my presence by anyone.

The wounds to my spinal cord occurred between my third and fourth vertebrae. Ashley elucidated on my specific condition. She said that I have a central cord syndrome, caused by damage to the central part of the spinal cord, a lesion in the gray matter of the cord. I also have Brown-Séquard syndrome. This is corruption to one half of the spinal cord, which affects the opposite side of the body; either the right or left side will experience paralysis, along with loss of sensation, pain, temperature sensation, and proprioception.[10] My right side is weaker, or more damaged, than my left.

A few weeks later, after this shock of information, William was sitting on my lap driving my wheelchair down the hallway, a favorite evening pastime for my kids. They'd take the controls and propel us around the third floor of the hospital. Once William got us jammed between two double doors. Gwyneth, who'd been running alongside of us, dashed to the nurses' station and told them that I was stuck. An amused nurse came to our rescue, and William and I continued on our merry way. When we reached the end of the corridor, a sign read: HANDICAP ACCESS ONLY. William pondered this for a moment. Handicap? "Mom, are you handicapped?" He uttered these words with the simple inquisitiveness of a young boy. And without giving me a chance to answer he added, in the forthright manner of a seven-year-old, "Oh, you're a quad." I gagged back the words "you're . . . a . . . quad" and tried to regain normal breathing.

When my family left, I went back to my room and the dam broke. My great-with-child nursing assistant Ashley held me as I sobbed. I did not want to be a quadriplegic. I did not want my children to think of me as "a quad."

For a long time, I couldn't utter the phrase, "I'm a quadriplegic," out loud. And even today, as I'm writing several years later, the audible hearing of the term quadriplegia sounds strange to my ears.

Many medical professionals presently use *tetraplegia*

instead. As aforementioned, it is now considered more accurate to use the Greek-Greek combination rather than the Latin-Greek combination, quadriplegia. But I wonder if the word quadriplegia tastes bitter in their mouths. Perhaps tetraplegia doesn't have the same jarring effect. Is it easier to tell someone she has tetraplegia rather than quadriplegia? The latter seems definitive and final, a diagnosis of damnation.

Tellingly, perhaps, my Word program doesn't even recognize the former term, underscoring it in red every time it is typed. *Tetraplegia* is unknown to most people, and therefore, creates a non-response. Some words shock or offend our senses. They sting; they cut. But I don't believe the best course of action is to change or avoid words that pierce.

Perhaps the most often avoided words are those associated with death. We do not want to say that someone "died," so we placate our senses with the more innocuous phrase "passed away." The problem to my mind, however, is that with death there is heartache. And oh how essential that we allow our hearts to indeed feel death's sting. If we do not feel the blade, then we need not be healed or comforted.

The victory of Jesus Christ over death is only ever tasted and known *in* the crucible of death, never apart from it. Similarly, the sweet comfort of our Lord is known in our honest, real pain. The pain of quadriplegia, cancer, and deformity. The pain of broken relationships and broken homes. The pain of death and the dying.

18

He had expected, as anyone might, that a giant would be monstrous. But in fact, it seemed to him that everything about the giant was exactly the right size and shape, and that he, Worvil, was abnormally small. He felt as if he were looking at the only real man in the world. That was a real eye, a real nose, a real mouth. His own were merely tiny shadows.

—Jennifer Trafton, *The Rise and Fall of Mount Majestic*

Gnosticism is an ancient heresy embraced during the second century. Its adherents, Gnostics, were "enlightened" sorts who rejected the material world and revered the spiritual world. Created material, they contended, including the body, is bad and, therefore, should be scorned. The soul and wisdom, they held, are good and, therefore, should be pursued.

This belief was declared heretical as God Himself declares creation is good. "And God saw everything that he had made, and behold, it was very good" (Gen. 1:31), and "For everything created by God is good, and nothing is to be rejected if it is received with thanksgiving" (1 Tim. 4:4). Jesus, God the Son, actually currently possesses a human body, thus attesting that our bodies are indeed good.

We've come a long way since our Gnostic predecessors. In fact, some might say we've fallen into a slough on the other side of the fence. Now, material *isn't* bad. Material is all there is, and thus, all that matters. As a result, we spend our time, energy, and money amassing stuff. Our bodies have become temples not for the living God but for our own personal aggrandizement and gratification. We worship at the temples of health, beauty, sex, fashion, and fitness. We seek to fill ourselves with the promises of these industries—assurances of significance, power, influence, glamour, and relevance. We've all been lured into the mire of misrepresented material.

But have Christians really evolved from the Gnosticism that once thwarted Christendom? Or have we reacted to the folly of our day in such a way that we have once again been thrust into the arms of this ancient heresy? Do we see material as good? Is the body good? Is there an underlying belief in Christian circles suggesting that "really spiritual" people don't care about their bodies, but instead are concerned with their souls, their spiritual lives?

Why did Jesus come? A common response to this query is that we need to be saved. Because of sin, we've been separated from our heavenly Father, and through faith in Jesus, we are reunited. But how? Through the perfect life of Jesus, the death He died for us as a just payment for our sin, and His subsequent resurrection. We could not save ourselves, so God Himself came to rescue and redeem His people. This is glorious, wonderful truth.

But why the incarnation? Why did God become human —flesh, blood, bones, muscles, sinews, nerves, a beating heart, breath, spinal cord, DNA? Gregory of Nazianzus, fourth century archbishop of Constantinople, illuminates for us the essentialness of Christ's body: "For that which He [Christ] has not assumed He has not healed; but that which is united to His Godhead is also saved."[11] Salvation begins with the incarnation. Jesus, dear friends, assumed a body, mind, and soul for the very reason that that is what needs to be healed: broken, diseased, dying bodies, threadbare, twisted minds, and disfigured, dark souls—these He gathers into Himself and by doing so, heals and redeems.

If you read the Gospels, you will discover that Jesus is bombarded by people seeking physical healing. And He never chides the sufferer, telling him that his focus is all wrong. Never does He redirect the sick or injured to get her priorities straight . . . to seek healing for her soul, not her flesh. He does indeed address the heart, but never at the expense of the body.

Both Matthew and Luke tell the story of some men who bring their paralytic friend to Jesus. When Jesus sees the faith of these men He says, "Your sins are forgiven." End of story? What happens next? Then Jesus said, "That's it. We're finished here. What you really needed was your soul to be restored. Now you're healed." Right? Of course not. Both gospels proclaim that after He forgives the men, He then heals the body of the paralytic.

> He said to the man who was paralyzed—"I say to you, rise, pick up your bed and go home." And immediately he rose up before them and picked up what he had been lying on and went home, glorifying God. And amazement seized them all, and they glorified God and were filled with awe, saying, "We have seen extraordinary things today." (Luke 5:24–26)

We have been created soul, mind, *and* body.

Our humanity is perceived in light of the giant, the true man, Jesus Christ. Jesus is the perfect human. And our humanity is only rightly grasped by knowing and looking to Him. Contrary to the popular notion that we define ourselves, we cannot even know ourselves apart from God. Blaise Pascal pondered this reality: "Not only do we only know God through Jesus Christ; we only know life and death through Jesus Christ. Apart from Jesus Christ we cannot know the meaning of our life or our death, of God or of ourselves."[12] There is no true knowledge worthy of that word apart from Him.

Scripture teaches that Jesus became fully man without

ceasing to be fully God. When we look to Jesus, we begin to understand and know the triune God. And when we look to Him we *also* begin to understand our own humanity.

PART THREE

the

miraculous

19

You never really understand a person until you
consider things from his point of view . . . until
you climb inside of his skin and walk around in it.

—Harper Lee, *To Kill a Mockingbird*

Over the next forty days at the rehabilitation hospital, I made, as John urged, a little bit of progress each day. Only some days, I was a little rebellious and then the progress was stunning. I remember John would arrive in the afternoon and I, with the giddiness of a child, would exclaim, "Guess what I did today!" or "Look what I can do now!"

I learned to maneuver my power wheelchair all by myself.

One day, I was slumped in my motorized metal chair getting ready for the nurse to transfer me to my bed, and I sat upright. It was really such a small movement of my core stomach muscles. Yet, the nurse and I looked at each other. Smiles and amazement.

"Did you see that?"

"Yes, that was awesome."

Those who had entered into my valley of suffering re-joiced with us over every infinitesimal bit of progress. Slowly I began to regain strength and ability in my legs. I began the task of crawling and learning to stand. My brain puzzled over how to do things that I'd been doing since I was a toddler. My therapists held a belt around my waist while I leaned on a tall walker and took awkward, halting steps. "Pick up this foot." "Shift your weight over your hip," they would tell me.

The ruptured relationship between my spinal cord and brain left me feeling vulnerable. I constantly thought I was going to fall headlong onto my face. Like a sparrow with a broken wing, I struggled, faltered, and dragged my wounded body across the floor. Oh how I missed the graceful fluidity I had once known. What a subtle wonder it is to walk! We don't even think about the intricate harmony playing between our spinal cord, brain, muscles, and nerves . . . the beauty of a single step . . . of a series of steps flowing together. We truly are fearfully and wonderfully made.

I gained arm strength and coordination, but my hands were quite another story. Ashley put rubber bands on my toiletries. I did not have normal sensation in my extremities and the rubber bands were additional grip and feedback for my brain. But no matter how hard I tried, I could not open my deodorant or lotion. I could not pull the tab to open my container of cereal or bend the carton to open the milk. I could not pull on my socks. Or brush my hair. Or hold a pen. Or open the cards flowing into the hospital. Or turn the pages of a book.

When you suffer a spinal cord injury, the question on everyone's mind is, "Will she ever walk again?" But I was wrestling with another reality. What if I can walk, but my hands never heal? What if in my clumsy way I learn to hold a toothbrush but will always need someone to open the toothpaste and squeeze it onto my toothbrush? Will I need someone to cut my food? To tie my shoelaces? To zip my zippers and buckle my belt?

And what about William and Gwyneth? Who will open the Play-Doh and help them sculpt food and tiny animals? Who will bake the cake for their birthdays or surprise them with cookies when they come home from school? Who will apply Band-Aids—to their skinned knees and scraped hearts? Who will brush the falling tears from their cheeks?

One day a woman from our church visited me in the hospital. She told me she was going to a prayer conference and asked how she could pray for me. I beseeched her to pray for my hands. That weekend, many gathered in prayer and asked the Lord to restore my hands.

My therapist Ashley said she wished she had videotaped my progress; never had she witnessed anything like it. The large therapy room contained a small mock grocery store off to the side. For a while, my arm would clumsily lunge for a piece of wax fruit, but I could not cajole my hand or fingers to wrap themselves around the apple. Soon after the prayer conference, however, my *right* hand surrendered to the desires and commands of my brain. As I am right-handed, this development was such a gift.

Now, as you may recall, my right side was the weaker, slower, less coordinated side of my body. My left side was, and still is, stronger, more reliable, and coordinated. But slowly I began to be able to pick up those pegs and place them in their little holes. Slowly I began to hold a pen. In childlike scrawl, I scratched the Scripture verses facing me across my hospital bed over and over again on a notepad.

If, at this point, dear reader, you're mystified or stupefied, astonished or in awe, then yes, you are beginning to grasp the rarity and wonder of these moments.

God was healing my body in a profound way. And in the process, He was showing His great glory. Nurses, therapists, doctors, friends, teachers, and lots of strangers reveled at the miraculous work unfolding before them.

When God is on the move, news travels. My surgeon heard the rumor that I was beginning to walk again; he was incredulous. He'd seen the damage up close—and I imagine a mangled spinal cord makes a lasting impression. I'm sure he'd seen many injuries like mine and was witness to the grim results. This "walking" was something he'd have to see for himself. He made a special trip from his workplace, driving to the rehabilitation hospital where I'd been transferred.

And my doctor did indeed find me on my feet, ambling down a long corridor, aided by my therapist. My arms leaned heavily on a high walking device, and I was haltingly, clumsily moving one foot forward, followed slowly by the shuffling of the other. It took all my physical strength and brain power. There was no flow or grace in the movement.

My walking was, in fact, quite ugly; yet the moment was magnificently beautiful. I was on my feet *moving*. I thanked Dr. Brown and told him he did good work.

Stunned, he grinned and replied, "I can take no credit. God did this."

20

Dear Friends,

On Friday May 29th, I injured my spinal cord. Twenty-six days have passed since then. I am so very thankful you are continuing to track my progress and are persevering with me in prayer. Your posts not only remind me that I've not been forgotten, but they strengthen my very core. It is so good to be remembered and loved by you all.

One of my most exciting progressions as of late is my ability to stand up (this, of course, is always done with supervision as I am still perfecting this maneuver). I have also been able to re-move my left wrist brace (prior to this, I have had braces on both hands because my wrists were too weak to support themselves). And I have learned to put in and take out my contact lenses by myself. That's some fine motor praise! ☺

I am grateful to be able to share new progress and yet, I must admit, am grieving the loss of my life prior to the accident. I had hopes and plans for the summer that I must surrender, in addition to normal everyday life. John told me that he and William cried for two hours on Father's Day as William recounted all the little things he missed about me. He has been an incredible boy through all of this. When I was telling him the other day how proud I am of him, he told me he thinks the accident has made him a better boy.

Gwyneth, my great little friend, is struggling in her own way. She feels a great sense of loyalty to me, which can be tough when others try to help. (This past school year, William was in school for a full day, so Gwyneth and I had lots of great one-on-one time. I simply adore that girl and we both miss each other terribly.)

I have a doctor who sometimes asks me if I have any words of wisdom. I don't see myself as the voice of wisdom, but I have thought a great deal lately about our fragility and amazing resilience. How one day you can be playing tag on a playground and the next day you are fighting to move your limbs. I have always loved the truth that God is mindful of our frames because quite honestly I am so weak. I've always been on the physically weaker side . . . for those who do not know me, I am a bit of a waif. But I was thinking more about how I am prone to wander, prone to leave the One I love. Thankfully, I am reminded by a verse posted on my hospital wall by one of my dear friends, "My grace is sufficient for you, for my power is made perfect in weakness" (2 Cor. 12:9). I go this day in the grace of my heavenly Father who strengthens my frail frame.

My fingertips are sore, so I'll say goodbye for now. Thank you again for persevering with me in this long journey.

Kate

21

Hello Friends,

This week has been yet another turn of good progress. I am now learning to take some steps during physical therapy with only the assistance of my therapists at my side. My rhythm and balance are slowly starting to come together. Relearning to walk is a very strange, awkward, and sometimes scary process. Therefore, I appreciate your continued prayers regarding this endeavor.

My therapists have set a goal for me to be walking safely by the end of the month. Being the overachiever that I am, I'm working hard to meet this challenge. My right arm is getting stronger. Up until a few days ago I had to wear an air splint on my right arm when doing arm exercises (otherwise my arm would lose control, and I would need assistance to get it back in place), but now I can control and move it as needed. And I no longer need to wear a neck brace!

On Tuesday I took a field trip to Blodgett Hospital to have my filter removed (I had this filter in place in order to catch any blood clots). The filter needed to be removed because if left in too long it would begin to attach to my body and would have become a permanent filter. All went well with this outpatient surgery. I even made it back in time for some physical therapy (despite the order that returned with me prohibiting exercise for forty-eight hours). I'm pretty hard-core when it comes to therapy!

Prior to my accident I would have been reasonably calm about this type of surgery. I must admit, however, I was a little nervous about the procedure. I have met several patients who are at Mary Free Bed as a result of a surgery gone wrong. However, I took a gift from a sister in Christ to Blodgett Hospital with me that was of great comfort. On Monday evening a friend from church brought dinner for us and before she left, she handed me a verse written on a little torn piece of paper. The verse read:

> The LORD directs the steps of the godly. He delights in every detail of their lives. Though they stumble, they will never fall, for the LORD holds them by the hand. (Ps. 37:23–24 NLT)

I memorized this precious gift Monday night and took the little torn piece of paper to the hospital with me Tuesday morning. What a comfort to know that God cares about every detail in my life. What a balm to my soul knowing that though I stumble, God holds me by the hand. My feet and heart do stumble every day, but I'm leaning heavily on the promise that my sweet Savior has hold of me.

Tomorrow (Saturday, the 4th of July) I am getting a day pass to go home. I have not been home since the day of the accident—May 29th—so I am very excited. Thank you again for your hearts of compassion and support.

Kate

22

Hello all. I hope this message finds you well.

For the 4th of July, I left the hospital for my first day pass home. Thank you all for your prayerswe had a wonderful day together, filled with a myriad of emotions. I joyfully sipped coffee at my kitchen table. I nervously watched my kids climb the willow tree in our backyard. We took a stroll down a nearby trail—I in a wheelchair and the kids on their bikes. I held my breath as Gwyneth navigated her bike down some hills; the tops of her shoes took a beating but she safely maneuvered down each dip in the path. Gwyneth and Will made several stops along the trail—Gwen to pick flowers for the pink basket on the front of her bike . . . Will to look for little creatures. William caught a toad and Gwyneth happily took the little prize for a ride in her basket. ☺ We ended the day with apple pie and returned to the hospital—my home away from home. In search of fireworks, we found a wing of the hospital with offices abandoned for the holiday and a corridor with floor to ceiling glass windows. We had a perfect view of the dark city as it was illuminated with blasts of color, and we could even hear each accompanying boom.

The kids and John are now in Kentucky (along with two of John's younger sisters and his brother-in-law—who happens to be a favorite uncle to Will and Gwen). Before the accident, we planned a camping trip to the Cumberland Gap—the kids are looking forward to hiking, swimming, catching salamanders, possibly horseback riding, and camping by the fire. Also, this is the only place in the Western Hemisphere where you can see a moonbow (a couple of days each month the moon makes a rainbow over Cumberland Falls), so this was another point of excitement. They are returning late Sunday evening.

Yesterday I received some stressful news and ask that you will pray for me. I had a tentative release date of July 22nd. This date, however, has been changed to next Tuesday, the 14th. This announcement came as a great shock to me and has been difficult on several levels. As I mentioned, John and the kids will not be returning until Sunday evening. This gives John only one day to switch our bedroom, which is currently located in the downstairs of our split-level duplex, with William's room. But perhaps what is even more difficult for me is that my physical therapist had set a goal that I would be walking safely and confidently before I returned home—I am doing neither yet. My physical therapist is on vacation and, therefore, was not present at the conference that led to the decision to change my discharge date.

A few weeks ago, Gwyneth asked John if it was okay for her to hope that I would someday walk again. I've been working hard and had hoped to come home as planned on two feet, without assistance. To be leaving with a walker or wheelchair is a great disappointment to me. As I type, I am conscious that this may seem a twinge ungrateful. Know that I feel tremendously blessed for every ounce of current and future progress. Yet I cannot help but feel like I have to some degree failed. Relearning to walk is undoubtedly one of the toughest challenges I have ever faced. I hope you will not feel compelled to convince me that I haven't failed. I just want to share what's stirring in my heart. Your kindness to me through the Care Page leaves me feeling safe to share what is true.

Please pray for me as my heart adjusts to this recent change and for the details of my discharge: that I would not go home a day sooner than God wills, that I will have peace with the final decision, that our home will be in order, that God will strengthen John, that I will be able to come for outpatient rehabilitation five days a week (a decision is going to be made on Monday regarding outpatient rehab).

My heavenly Father has promised to hold me by the hand—in the darkness and disappointment, through my sorrow, in victory and defeat.

I pray this truth will sustain both you and me in these next days.

In the love and hope of Christ,

Kate

23

I don't believe that grief passes away. It has its time and place forever. More time is added to it; it becomes a story within a story. But grief and griever alike endure.

—Wendell Berry, *Jayber Crow*

Job is a man in the Bible with a massive tale of woe. He was a good man, blameless and upright, and he was an exceedingly rich man: "the greatest of all the people of the east" (Job 1:3). He was a father who loved and cared deeply for the souls of his seven sons and three daughters.

But alas, as the story goes, Satan strips Job of everything; well almost everything. In one deplorable day, his live-stock—*thousands* of animals—are annihilated or taken by enemies. And *all* his sons and daughters are killed under the collapsing roof of a house. At the catastrophic news, Job tears his clothes, shaves his head, and—take note—worships God. "Naked I came from my mother's womb," Job cries, "and naked shall I return. The LORD gave, and the LORD has taken away; blessed be the name of the LORD" (1:21).

As this was neither the response Satan expected or desired, the virulent viper persists in his affliction, this time with a blight of boils and sores. He torments Job, "from the sole of his foot to the crown of his head" (2:7). Three friends hear of the dark calamity that has fallen upon Job and travel from afar to see him. Their initial response should cause us all to pause. Scripture tells us that when they saw Job, so great was his suffering, they didn't even recognize him. And here is the part that prompts my pause:

> And they raised their voices and wept, and they tore
> their robes and sprinkled dust on their heads toward
> heaven. And they sat with him on the ground seven
> days and seven nights, and no one spoke a word to him,
> for they saw that his suffering was very great. (2:12)

They wept. They settled in the dust and dirt. And for seven days and seven nights, they said nothing. They were just with him . . . in his grief. Oh, that we too might embrace one another in grief. That we might settle in the dirt of one another's lives. That we might share tears. That we might sit side by side and absorb the shock wave of sorrow together.

But this, of course, is not a happy, comfortable place. It is not easy to imbibe the turmoil of another. Job's flesh is rotting and infested with worms. The death of his children is fresh. His wife is bitter. His shame is massive.

People's reactions to great suffering and grief are so vast

that they could, and probably have been, explored in countless books. But I have perceived two pervasive responses in our culture that seem to influence and dominate how we react to grief.

The first treats grief as an unwelcome, uninvited trespasser to be shunned or dismissed. Note that when Job's friends saw him, none of them uttered today's go-to verse, a verse imparted too readily with too little understanding: "And we know that for those who love God all things work together for good, for those who are called according to his purpose" (Rom. 8:28). This is a wonderful and precious truth, one that can act as a balm to the sufferer.

Yet this verse is often uttered less as a poultice and more as a form of escapism. It's as if we are saying, "Let's not dwell on this bad. We don't really even need to be sad. Give thanks. God is going to do something good here, don't you see?" Dear reader, what of grief? What of lament? Are we giving thanks, when instead we should be letting our hearts break? Too often, uncomfortable with pain, we simply want to skip it, smother it, or shield ourselves from its annoying awkwardness. Rather than look in the face of suffering, we cast our glance aside, forge a smile, and deny the stench and horror so obviously before us; we play a game of make-believe, granting our hearts permission not to split but persuading them to calcify.

The gospel of John tells a story with which many are familiar. Lazarus, a dear friend of Jesus, becomes sick. Jesus does not immediately travel to see His ailing friend, but instead arrives several days later. He knows by this time Lazarus is dead. Lazarus's sisters, Mary and Martha, have buried their brother in a tomb and after mourning for four days, are worn and weary.

When Jesus arrives, He is first met outside the village by Martha. And when Mary is summoned, she falls, rife with grief, at the feet of Jesus, weeping. How does her Lord respond? Does He tell her, "Don't worry. No need to cry. I purposely came late so that Lazarus could die and be raised, so you could see My awesome power, so you would know that I am the One"?

Jesus knows exactly what He's come to do. And, indeed, it's going to be good; it's going to stagger and stun; it's going to usher in incalculable joy. In just a few moments with just a few words, He will impel a rotting corpse back to life. Tears of mourning will be turned to tears of jubilance.

But don't miss this. The apostle John grants us passage to something of the utmost importance. He remembers that upon seeing Mary, Jesus was, "deeply moved in his spirit and greatly troubled" (John 11:33). And then John tells us that Jesus began to weep (v. 35). We would be wise to linger over these sweet words. Dear reader, we must see and taste and feel the tears falling down Jesus' face. We must hear the guttural cry of our Lord. He suffers His heart to bleed and break. And so must we.

In just a few minutes, Jesus is going to turn death on its

head. Couldn't He have skipped the tears? But He doesn't, does He? Jesus weeps. He enters into their grief because they are entering His grief. Here Jesus Christ, the life and light of the world, is affronted by death and darkness. Mary and Martha have swallowed back the bitter dregs of death and in doing so have tasted the sorrow of their Lord, the One who made them for His glory but are living under the crushing weight of the sin-filled world. Jesus' disciple shows us that not only are we are joined to *one another* in our grief, we are united *to Jesus* in His.

I mentioned that there were two responses to grief that I wanted to sift. The second response is to treat grief not as a foe but as a friend, a codependent lover. In this case, the griever does not shun grief, but instead coddles it, dotes on it, gives it a position of authority in his life. Grief is indulged at every opportunity. I cannot do my schoolwork because I am grieving. I cannot see your pain because I am so enamored with my own. I cannot be held responsible to complete this task because I am going through a hard time.

To be sure, grief can and does, at times, bring us to our knees. And yet eventually, even in our grief, we must rise. The children still need to be fed, the bills must be paid, the laundry cleaned, the grass cut. Resilience is one of the great virtues of the Christian life. To the war-torn people of Germany, on the heels of a devastating air raid, Helmut Thielicke wrote,

To these wounds of the innermost man, [God] says:
"Thy sins are forgiven thee." The other wounds of life
are those inflicted by destiny and suffering, by sickness
and poverty, by violence of war, by force, and by the
sorrow of this world which constantly makes us home-
less within it. To this hurt of tormented humanity Jesus
says, "Rise, take up thy bed and walk."[13]

We are called to live with strength and courage of heart. A
shadow may exist over our joy. But it cannot make us forever
numb to joy.

In another story penned by the apostle John, he bids
us enter into the tale of a man who had been crippled for
thirty-eight years. When Jesus and His disciples encounter
this man, he is lying near a pool among many other invalids
waiting for someone to place him in the healing waters. But
alas, when the waters stir, someone else always beats him
to it. Jesus sees this man and asks him, "Do you want to be
healed?" (see John 5:1–15). Isn't the answer to the question
obvious? That's why he's there, right? But perhaps this is not
a rhetorical question.

Are we ourselves content with lives of sorrow and sin?
Has pain made a permanent dwelling place in our hearts,
become a pleasant and satisfying companion? Are we
competitively counting our crosses and comparing our
wounds with each other? Would we rather blog at the
computer continually reminding others and ourselves that

we are wounded or, dear friends, do we want to taste and see that the Lord is good?

Do we want to be healed?

Though grief remains a part of us, we should not need nor should we desire to be continually affirmed in our sadness. That doesn't mean we won't sometimes speak of our sorrow or that we won't continue to grieve. Some wounds we bear until heaven. It merely means that grief takes its proper place in our stories, and its role is never that of the star, nor does it play the part of the savior.

We live in the shadow, dear reader, but the darkness cannot overcome the light.

24

Nothing is ever finished and done with in this world.
You may think a seed was finished and done with when it
falls like a dead thing into the earth; but when it puts forth
leaves and flowers next spring you see your mistake.

—Elizabeth Goudge, *The Little White Horse*

After forty days at the rehabilitation hospital, I was released from the hospital with a cane (which I couldn't really hold very well but it alerted people around me to be careful). A huge banner painted with polka dots spanned the garage: "WELCOME HOME KATE!" And more happy signs adorned the outside of our duplex. I was home. I would have to return to Mary Free Bed five days a week for therapy, but I was home.

That night I climbed into bed with Gwyneth. Lying next to her *in her bed* felt so good. She narrowed her wide sea-green eyes and fixed her gaze on me. She didn't say anything. She didn't have to. Her happy, sad eyes said it all. Still to this day, she gives me this prolonged, penetrating stare and tells me with just a look that she loves me.

I was ever so thankful to be home, yet I missed the stability and safety that came with being surrounded by specialists. Now I was bombarded with reminders of things I could not do. Gwyneth stood outside the shower. As I sat in a chair with water running over me, she would open the shampoo, conditioner, or soap and squirt it into my hand. She was, and still is, my fierce, stalwart helper.

Meals now came to our door from that ever-increasing community of friends. My mom lived with us for a while, driving me to therapy and helping with the kids. John's family bought us a freezer and filled it with ready-made meals.

The first Sunday after my release from the hospital, with hearts full of anticipation, we traveled to Church of the Servant, to worship alongside the body of believers who'd loved us so thoroughly over the tumultuous days since my fall. Together with our brothers and sisters in Jesus Christ, we worshiped the God who sees, a Father who heals.

As a living testimony of His goodness and power, I stood. I lifted my voice. I hung on to every word of my pastor Jack Roeda's preaching. And in a most beautiful display, we joined the Communion circle gathered around the table at the front of the church.

As the climax of the church service, congregants would file out of their rows and come forward, forming a circle where the bread and wine would be passed. Each participant would first receive the Eucharist, and then would pass the host and the cup to the next person. When all had partaken, the communicants would withdraw from the circle and return to their chairs while a new circle would be formed. This continued until all persons had a chance to come forward and receive. With my cane hooked over my arm, I waited for the bread to pass. John directed and fixed his eyes on mine testifying, "This is the body of Christ, Kate, broken for you." The cup followed. "The blood of Christ. Shed for you." As he held the goblet, I dipped the bread into the wine. Then he passed the cup for me, and I spoke these same words to the person next to me.

I think all eyes were on us. The beauty of the moment was more than we could comprehend. The Holy Spirit hovered among us. We cast our doubts and fears, our sin and sadness, on the Lord.

We celebrated a broken body being reclaimed and rebuilt for His glory.

25

"Why did you do all this for me?" he asked.
"I don't deserve it. I've never done anything for you."
"You have been my friend," replied Charlotte.
"That in itself is a tremendous thing."

—E. B. White, *Charlotte's Web*

When you ascend the steps to the upper level of our home, you might notice two sizable black-and-white photographs—gifts that bedeck the wall. The first—a picture of William and me standing side by side. With self-assured hands on hips and happy eyes, my then seven-year-old beams. The crook of my arm rests on his head, elbow bent; I'm playfully leaning on my son. The portrait next to us is a close-up of a round-headed four-year-old, big eyes, knowing smile. The astute observer would note that cradling her neck is an arm . . . that belongs to me, her mom.

Within a moment's time, you would see the likenesses: Gwyneth takes after her daddy (I like to call her the little Swede and him the big Swede) and William, in appearance, takes after me. William and Gwyneth are the very flesh and blood of John and me. We are joined. Bonded. Family.

Something similar, but far grander still, happened with the miracle of the incarnation. Jesus broke into the cosmos, becoming bone of our bone and flesh of our flesh, so that we might have new life by being drawn into *His* beautiful life, the very life and love He has forever shared with His Father in the communion of the Holy Spirit. Jesus, swaddled in our flesh, came for us as one of us—to heal our broken minds, to mend our sin-sick hearts, to restore our fragile bodies.

The Christian is united to Jesus. Joined. Bonded. Family.

And not only is the Christian joined to Christ, Christians are thereby joined to one another. Scripture refers to Christians as the very body of Christ, the church. To one another, we are joined. Bonded. Yes, family. Never did I experience what it meant to be a part of Christ's body—or family— more than when I was physically broken.

To be sure, we had known the sweetness of the church. As mentioned earlier, when I was six months pregnant with William, the doctor discovered that William's heart rate was crazy fast—450 beats a minute fast. We were living in Dallas, Texas, at the time, more than a thousand miles from any family. This was before the explosion of social media. Nonetheless, word travels fast in the Christian community. Soon saints all across the States—people we had never met and will likely never meet this side of heaven—were swaddling our unborn son in prayer.

That's how it is with the church. We enter into one another's suffering and fight for one another. We do this because we are of one Spirit and one body. The apostle Paul teaches us:

There is one body and one Spirit—just as you were called to the one hope that belongs to your call—one Lord, one faith, one baptism, one God and Father of all, who is over all and through all and in all. (Eph. 4:4–6)

When my accident happened about seven years after William's brush with death, our family began to live again on the prayers and care of the saints. We had no biological family in Grand Rapids, and we had just a few friends—our best friends had moved a year prior to the fall. But Christians are the adopted sons and daughters of God, joined in heart. We had brothers and sisters in Jesus Christ all around us who loved us with the sacrificial love of family.

We did not deserve the kindness lavished on us, for we did not even know most of the people who prayed, visited, baked, wrote, and gave to our family. I cannot even claim, as in the quote above from *Charlotte's Web*, that I had been a friend first—or ever! To be a friend to a stranger is an exceptionally tremendous thing, and we experienced this again and again.

As John was a full-time student then, and I only working

part-time, we did not have insurance through our employers. We felt strongly, however, that it would be unwise and unfaithful not to have some type of health insurance, so we purchased an out-of-pocket plan—to cover us in case something "catastrophic" might happen. Funny, right?

When something catastrophic did indeed happen, we got an opportunity to test the waters of this plan. Let's just say the water was brisk and sparse; we were soon left dry and parched, accumulating debt by the minute. The insurance would only cover thirty days of rehabilitation. The doctors at Mary Free Bed gave me a scholarship so I could stay an extra ten days. Yet upon release, our insurance would cover no outpatient therapy. Since I needed daily therapy at a specialized spinal cord program, the bills, as you can imagine, began to multiply and swell . . . and swell some more.

Soon after my injury, a few of my dearest friends realized that the necessary care was going to be far beyond our reach financially. One of them contacted the founder of the charter school where our kids attended. She asked him—a Christian—if he'd be willing to help her with a fundraiser. He told her he wasn't very good at organizing fundraisers, but what he was good at was writing checks. He contacted my home church and set up a fund to help with the medical costs. Another friend set up a PayPal account where donations could be made (this was before the time of GoFund-Me) for other daily living essentials.

My friends then joined forces with our church. In October, five months after the injury, they held a spaghetti dinner for our family. The charter school community, our church community, anyone and everyone was invited to come hear my story and donate to the medical fund. On that blustery autumn day, we arrived at the church. My dad was concerned and perhaps a little skeptical that people would want to leave the warmth of their homes. Would anyone actually come? Would anyone want to give? We were overwhelmed with the response. Confounded, my dad said, *"I didn't even know people like this existed."*

My dad served as a corpsman in the Navy and Marines. Little did he know that to be part of the church—the body of Christ—is to have your own personal battalion. When a brother or sister falls, an army rushes to the front line; they fight the fight their stricken brother cannot. They hoist their injured sister over their shoulder, carrying her broken body in prayer to the Great Physician. They bear a family resemblance to their heavenly Father and Brother, Jesus, sacrificing for those to whom they have been bonded—a family of faith, the holy church. The tables at our church were filled with strangers, strangers who were also very much family. A family bonded in the truth: "If one member suffers, all suffer together; if one member is honored, all rejoice together" (1 Cor. 12:26).

PART FOUR

the light

26

I would always rather be happy than dignified.

—Charlotte Brontë, *Jane Eyre*

Jane Eyre is perhaps one of the finest female characters in all of literature. But if you're familiar with her tale, you will remember Jane as being quite dignified. She is an orphan, but she unabashedly shares her thoughts with those in authority. She is cast off by her aunt and treated cruelly during her orphan days, yet she is neither diffident nor feeble.

Twice she refuses to enter into marriage—in the first instance, she loves and is deeply loved by another. But she discovers some staggering news on her wedding day (spoiler alert) and will not join herself to someone who is already wed (even if the circumstances of her fiancé's marriage were treacherous). Jane is a mighty little wisp of dignity and self-respect. Though tortured in spirit and tempted to go through with the ceremony, she concludes, "I will respect myself. I will keep the law given by God; sanctioned by man.

I will hold to the principles received by me when I was sane, and not mad—as I am now."

With the second proposal of marriage, she resists the despotic pressure to marry another out of duty rather than for love.

Dignified. Passionate. Mournful. Expressive. High-spirited. Serious. Noble. Each of these adjectives describes Jane. Happy, on the other hand, is not the defining word that springs to mind for the character whose story is indelibly marked with sorrow. And yet curiously inserted into this tale is the brief phrase, "I would always rather be happy than dignified." Dear Jane, what are you trying to tell me?

There is little dignity associated with the inability to perform tasks necessary for daily living or care. As mentioned previously, I was grateful when a family member was present when it was time to eat. And for the most part, the staff at the rehabilitation hospital was amazing. But I have seared in my mind a few nails-on-chalkboard moments. One time, I recall someone whose body language effectively communicated that she was not too thrilled about being assigned to help me eat. She put the chicken sandwich near my mouth, and I took a bite. While I was rapidly chewing, she continued to hold the sandwich, utterly bored and clearly irritated. I tried to make small talk (which is hard to do when you're scarfing down food), but she was unresponsive. Embarrassed, I wished my hospital bed would swallow me whole.

But even when a staff member whom I loved came to feed me, the situation was awkward. The mission was to get the food eaten. Talking interrupted such progress. I felt guilty for not being able to feed myself, for occupying the staff's valuable time, as I knew they had other work to do.

On a separate occasion, one of the paramedics who had transferred me to the rehabilitation hospital came to visit and brought a friend to meet me. I was sitting in my wheelchair feeling pretty cheerful. I was humbled to have so many strangers visit me. Apparently, I was a fascinating subject of conversation among the paramedics—few people I suppose are so severely bested on a playground. After a short chat, they left. I looked down to find my Depends sticking out of my workout pants. This discovery left me feeling neither happy nor dignified.

Sometimes I felt I had been stripped of all dignity, naked and ashamed. Yet something peculiar happens to those struck with tragedy or sickness. Truth enters and pretense fades. We've all, to varying degrees, experienced this. Have you ever found yourself sick with the flu, on your hands and knees, not even caring that your face is mere inches from the toilet? You're so miserable you lose all semblance of refinement. All you want is to get the vomit out of your system and into the toilet so you can feel better. Similarly, those who are battling sickness in the hospital become less concerned about the thin gown and their disheveled hair.

There are moments in life when we must all come to

terms with our smallness and fragility. Moments of truth when our hearts are recalibrated. Trifling anxieties and fears we've been collecting and hoarding lose their color. Folly is laid bare. The shallows of our heart make way for the deep. Our need for mercy and for someone to come and rescue us is brought into the light. In these moments, we are not, as some might presume, ashamed. Quite the opposite. Shedding the falsehood of autonomy and self-sufficiency, we can receive the love of Jesus and of others.

The Skin Horse in the children's tale *The Velveteen Rabbit* illumines for us this process of what he calls becoming "Real."

> It doesn't happen all at once. . . . You become. It takes a long time. That's why it doesn't happen often to people who break easily, or have sharp edges, or who have to be carefully kept. Generally, by the time you are Real, most of your hair has been loved off, and your eyes drop out and you get loose in the joints and very shabby. But these things don't matter at all, because once you are Real you can't be ugly, except to people who don't understand.[14]

The author of Hebrews tells us that Jesus, "for the joy that was set before him endured the cross, despising the shame, and is seated at the right hand of the throne of God" (Heb. 12:2). What if Jesus had placed dignity above brokenness? If He had claimed His right to be right? If He had chosen to unleash just judgment rather than allow His naked body to be exposed for all to see lifted high on a cross, bearing the crushing weight of our iniquity, the filthy shame of our sin?

Jesus could have rejected the suffering and humiliation of the cross. Yet He knew there was a flood of joy that would follow and swallow His and our shame. He chose this joy over respectability, above what the world perceives as greatness and strength. He chose to die that we might live. To be ripped asunder from the Father that we might be rejoined, that we might be regrafted into the triune family. Perhaps our beloved Jane Eyre took her cue from someone bolder and wiser than she.

What a good day it will be when with finality we shed our cloaks of insecurity and fear. When we no longer restrain our joy for fear of appearing undignified. When we cease to shelter ourselves in feigned moral virtue, but rather lap up every drop of happiness offered us. Oh that we might know the freedom of singing, and laughing, and dancing with a full heart, unhinged from pride and vanity. That we might yield our self-designed disguises and taste the cheer of pure, authentic, bona fide friendship.

27

Some nights in the midst of this loneliness I swung among the
scattered stars at the end of the thin thread of faith alone.

—Wendell Berry, *Jayber Crow*

I was loved. But sometimes, even when you're deeply
and profoundly loved, your heart aches with loneliness.
Sometimes the Enemy whispers that you are alone in your
pain. There is a measure of truth to his sinister murmurings;
the Adversary always mingles that which is false with a
thread of truth. Pain does separate.

I wish I could share, just for a moment, the nerve pain
peeling through my hands, down my left side, and into my feet
with John so that he could say, "Ah, I see. Now I know what
you are facing." The pain is unrelenting, but I almost never
speak of it. I do not want my kids to be ever cognizant of this
burden, nor dampen their joy with the weight of my suffering.

I prefer to avoid the awkwardness in conversations that
typically follows the admittance that indeed, I am at this
very moment hurting. Pain tempts us to push others away.

You are alone in this, the lie resounds. My pain is different from John's fatigue and fear, is different from the torment and ache in William's heart, is different from Gwyneth's worry and woe. We suffer uniquely and at different times. My heart is happy this morning while yours is weak and afraid. You are burdened with a memory, and I am oblivious. I am crestfallen while you are content. Our sadness and joy do not align.

Though our unique stories of suffering isolate, they also bond. We image—emulate and reflect—Jesus by entering the shame and suffering of one another. When you hold someone who is desperate with pain, your hearts become interwoven. When the silence is broken, you invite me into your world. Your secret sadness becomes our shared sorrow.

The gospel truth refutes the lie of our Enemy. Our heavenly Father sent His Son in the power of the Holy Spirit. The Son became incarnate and, 2 in doing so, joined Himself to our pain. We are not alone. Jesus Christ is bonded body and soul to our broken lives. He suffers with us, but He is not a mere sympathizer. He doesn't join our pain as just another fellow sufferer, so as to give company to misery; He enters in as healer and redeemer.

We each wrestle with living a life that isn't quite the way it's supposed to be, a life marred by pain and sin. But we have not been abandoned—we are not wayfarers bereft of consolation.

One night I lay in bed suffering and feeling a kindredness

with Wendell Berry's character Jayber Crow. I was having trouble with my breathing. In a dark room under the vault of a black night I questioned, "Do You see me, Lord? I'm struggling to breathe. I feel like I'm dying."

―――――――――

I awoke on William's eighth birthday—his first since my injury—with a pounding headache still struggling to breathe. Yet I did not want to rob my boy of this once-a-year celebratory joy. William chose the movie *Where the Wild Things Are* to see with his visiting aunt and uncle. When we'd heard Maurice Sendak's story was coming to life on the big screen, we were curiously excited. This childhood favorite had been read so many times in our home, I can still today recite much of it by heart. I put on a cheerful face and braced myself against the pain resounding in my body.

After the movie, we went to the seafood restaurant William had chosen. By this time, I was taking short, labored breaths. I sat in the booth with our family, but ordered no food. I could not eat, as I was solely focused on getting breath. The adults deftly balanced worry for me with determination that William have a good time. The last five months of this boy's life had been laden with chaos and pain. We felt immense pressure to give this boy a day where he could feel happy and loved. I knew I was miserably failing him.

My hands trembled; the music and loud voices made my

head swim; my body was drunk with pain. By God's mercy, I survived the dinner without vomiting or fainting. My brother-in-law steadied me as we exited the restaurant—I was sure patrons watching thought I'd partaken in too much drink—and helped me to the car. We drove home and, with each passing moment, my fear increased.

John swiftly tucked William and Gwyneth into bed and drove me to an emergency clinic; his sister and brother-in-law stayed home with our kids. The doctors were befuddled about the cause of my symptoms. I asked them to take a sample of my urine. The laboratory results revealed a urinary tract infection, which can be fatal to a quadriplegic.

My occupational therapist Ashley had taught me about autonomic dysreflexia, a syndrome suffered by patients with spinal cord injuries at or above the sixth thoracic vertebrae located in the upper back. Since my injury is between the third and fourth cervical vertebrae in the neck, I am at risk for this condition. Autonomic dysreflexia, or AD, is threateningly high blood pressure resulting from pain or discomfort. If uncontrolled, it can lead to a stroke. In a spinal cord injury patient, it has several triggers: an overfull bladder or bowel, an infection in the kidney or bladder, pressure sores, ingrown toenails, cuts, burns, hot or cold temperatures, or blisters.[15] I still carry a medical alert card in my wallet explaining the risks and treatments for AD.

On Monday, I told Ashley about my symptoms; she immediately guessed the root of the problem. I was now more cognizant of the thin thread of life able to break at any moment. In this fragile state, the Enemy bid me believe that I'd been cast among the stars, alone, forgotten. But my heavenly Father has a word about His celestial lights:

> Lift up your eyes on high and see:
> who created these?
> He who brings out their host by number,
> calling them all by name;
> by the greatness of his might
> and because he is strong in power,
> not one is missing. (Isa. 40:26)

Not one is missing. *I am always near to you* is the word of the Father to His children. Threadbare though our faith at times may be, He is powerful to heal and help and hold His own.

28

Anne always remembered the silvery, peaceful beauty and
fragrant calm of that night. It was the last night before sorrow
touched her life; and no life is ever quite the same again when
once that cold, sanctifying touch has been laid upon it.

—L. M. Montgomery, *Anne of Green Gables*

Ever since I was a young child, and even still today, I
cannot get past the jolting truth that in a moment all of
life can change.

I still feel nauseated when I read the narrator's account
from *A Separate Peace* when he, in a split second, decides
to jounce the tree limb, resulting in his friend Finny's
devastating fall. I'm still heartsick when I read the account of
how Moses, out of anger, strikes the rock and God tells him
he will not be permitted to enter the Promised Land. After
forty years of enduring the craggy, harsh wilderness, Moses
sets his eyes but not his feet upon Canaan. His whining,
faint-of-heart people inherit God's promise of a home. I am
maddened when Digory from *The Magician's Nephew* twists

Polly's arm and rings the bell, which results in the awakening of the White Witch.

And I am moved as I remember William's troubled four-year-old heart when he saw a tormented woman on television sharing her story about how she hit and killed a cyclist with her car. For days, in his wee little voice, William prayed God would comfort that dear woman.

All these stories, of course, harken back to a pivotal moment in history—when Eve changes the trajectory of all our lives with one unfaithful taste of forbidden fruit in the garden.

———————

Our kids attended a charter school, and as part of their education, the school incorporated a "Moral Focus" curriculum—each month the students focused on a different character trait, such as wisdom, respect, gratitude, compassion, and so on.

In September, the children focused on the character trait of wisdom. They were taught the definition—to be careful to do what is right—and then given some key words linked with wisdom. We exercise wisdom when we *listen* very carefully, *think* very carefully, and then make good *choices* so we can be *responsible.*

At the end of each month, an assembly was organized. One class presented the character trait, and a student from each elementary class who exemplified this character trait received an award. William had sprouted into a second grader, and this year his class was in charge of presenting Wisdom. He asked John and me if we would come to the assembly.

We sat in plastic seats under fluorescent lights while the kids crisscrossed their legs, squishing into tight lines on the floor. William's class stood at the front of the bright yellow music room. They held large signs featuring the key words that describe wisdom: LISTEN, THINK, CHOOSE, RESPONSIBLE.

Blond hair and summer tan, apple-red T-shirt, William chanted in harmony with his class the definition of wisdom: to be careful to do what is right. Then the big moment arrived. If your name was called, you would make your way to the front of the room, look into the eyes of the principal (this was non-negotiable), shake his hand and, with your other hand, behold your prize—a yellow certificate. The ceremony was a gaiety of elated children rising, agilely tiptoeing over other students, and fast walking to the front of the room.

I was not expecting what I heard. When the boy's name was called, it came crashing over my head. And there before me, with a huge smile on his face, stood the child who'd caused my injury holding for all to see the certificate for Wisdom. The irony of it all was too much for me. Tears brimmed. As covertly as possible, John adeptly escorted me out of the room. By the time we reached the parking lot, the levy of sorrow broke; a torrent of tears and sobs convulsed from deep within my body.

The blitz of tears continued on my bed when we got home. John, my scholar and confidant, listened patiently. I think I can honestly say that I was never angry with the boy who had landed on me. I harbored no bitterness. But I *was* profoundly sad, especially on this day. Here I was struggling to tie my shoes and the boy responsible for my injury was being praised for his wisdom. I don't imagine this boy knew or fully understood what followed his jump. How could he? He was only a child.

I was raising children who loved—who *still* delight in—climbing. The loftier the tree, the better. Anne of Green Gables would approve of Gwyneth's pleasure in climbing into the sky and nestling into the branch of our old maple with a book in hand. When exiting, would either of my kids take the flying leap into the abyss, or would they follow the safe path of descent? Would they make impulsive decisions that would change the course of their lives . . . the course of others' lives? And if so, how would they and others react?

I certainly don't think the child who landed on me intended to hurt anyone. Perhaps the teacher who selected him for this particular award wanted to bless him—to redeem the past by conceiving a bright way forward; if that was the case, then I genuinely respect that decision. Who of us would not like to rewind the clock on some moments in our lives?

But the reality is that we can only live our lives forward and I, myself, have found regret and forgiveness to be great teachers. God not only bears the pain and sorrow that follows disastrous choices, He delights in redeeming our failures, mishaps, and calamities—great and small. Rather than leaving us to flounder in shame and guilt, He rebuilds and heals, defining us in and by His love.

But, of course, moments don't always result in a change for the worse. Our hearts cheer when Anne Shirley finally realizes she has always only loved Gilbert Blythe. When the brave Old Testament figure Ruth decides to stay with her mother-in-law after the death of her husband rather than return to her homeland of Moab, we are invited into the beautiful and powerful, a true tale of God's provision and love. Angels hold their breath while the hope of humanity stirs in that sacred moment when Jesus, the Son of God, humbles Himself, becoming hidden in the womb of a young teenage girl, teeny-tiny, curled up, floating, weak and vulnerable.

Thirty-three years later, in another profound and holy moment, the crucified Son of God, lifeless and breathless, raises from death, this time delivering death its very own fatal blow.

And the moment one's heart receives the forgiving love of Jesus Christ, life is forever altered. Once alienated from his heavenly Father, the prodigal child is embraced in the life and love of Jesus Christ.

Someday there will come a moment when Jesus returns to confront the Enemy that presently roams and torments the earth. In all His goodness and glory, Jesus will vanquish the serpent, putting a definitive end to his slithering ways. Jesus will overcome the darkness not in an epic battle but in the space of a moment. The sturdy old hymn "A Mighty Fortress Is Our God," penned by Martin Luther, expresses this truth. Hear the words of the third stanza:

> And though this world, with devils filled,
>   should threaten to undo us,
> We will not fear, for God hath willed His truth
>   to triumph through us:
> The Prince of Darkness grim, we tremble
>   not for him;
> His rage we can endure, for lo! his doom is sure,
> One little word shall fell him.

One little word. That is all it will take. My heart grieves the darkness, sorrow, and pain pressing from all sides in my life and in the world around me, yet one little word from our Father shall collapse the darkness, shall rout and put to flight the grim shadow of sin and sadness.

Jesus, swaddled in flesh, came for us as one of us—to heal our broken minds, to mend our sin-sick hearts, to restore our fragile bodies. We are not alone in the shadow. He redeems those moments that come crashing in, threatening to undo us. He bears the instances when we have fatally erred, when we've jounced the limb of a friend or twisted the arm of someone we love. He has borne our pain and sin so that we might be restored and re-created body and soul.

When our hope and delight is found in the one little Christmas babe, we are united to the one powerful resurrected King who promises at the right moment in time to return and utter a word able to vanquish all that is false and afflicts, to dispel the darkness with His light, beauty, and goodness. Dear friends, He is, at this moment, hemming us in to the life He shares with the Father and the Spirit.

He calls us not to implement and excel in a mere "moral focus," but to press into the very fullness and meaning of life, life Himself, Jesus Christ.

29

When our daughter Gwyneth was born she had full lung capacity. Unlike her brother, who was born two months premature and was immediately placed on a ventilator without uttering a sound, Gwyneth had a voice. A voice that echoed so forcibly across the maternity operating room that our obstetrician implored someone to "please shut that baby up" as she couldn't concentrate on my stitching amid the ear-piercing dirge of our daughter.

Not only did Gwyneth have her voice from the moment of her birth, she also began to put words together at a young age. By fifteen months, she could form short sentences. And ever since, we have been blessed with that singsongy voice.

With many words also came the desire to communicate, to be known, understood. Gwyneth would often delve into that dictionary in her head, endeavoring to share her feelings and thoughts. So it didn't surprise John too much when one day, not long after the accident, she said to her daddy, "I know that God is good. But He also seems mean. Why do mommies get hurt? And why did *my* mommy have to get hurt?" William was horrified by the seemingly impertinent question, exclaiming, "You can't say that!" I'm sure he was thinking, *You cannot say that God is mean and you certainly can't say it out loud.*

Several months after I was released from the hospital, I successfully passed my driver's test. (Before climbing back into a vehicle, I had to demonstrate that my brake reflexes were adequate, which I did using specialized equipment at the rehabilitation office. Then I had to take some road tests. Once again, I felt thrust back into history—like a teen full of trepidation when merging onto the highway and crossing lanes of traffic.) I was traveling one day with my little Gwyneth after building up some driving confidence, and she confided, "Mom."

I looked into the rearview mirror. "Yes?"

"I liked you better before the accident, before you got hurt."

Crack went my heart, tears started in my eyes. I returned a smile to her. "Yes, I know what you mean, Gwyneth. I agree."

I'm not who I was. When a doctor told my husband a week after my injury that I was not and would never be the same woman, he was right. I was not and would never be the same wife or the same mom. I'm not saying that I couldn't be a good wife and mom—just that I wasn't the same. And that still is a source of grief—in my life as well as the lives of those who love me.

In the early aftermath of my injury a fear began to worm its way into my heart—a fear I still contend with today—that I had become a disappointment and a burden. We are all, in reality, a combination of burden and blessing. Of course, we hope that the latter triumphs over the former but, sadly, this is often not the case.

Once capable and reliable, now I was clumsy and awkward. Once strong and quick, I was now weak, hindered by pain and fatigue. Once adventurous, now lame, disqualified from anything risky. This was not the woman I wanted to be. I still live with a fear that my kids will look back on their childhoods and remember all the things I could not do, that they'll recall the times when Mom stayed behind while everyone else forged ahead. That the sorrow they felt when Mom couldn't participate would resurface alongside memories of their adventures, casting a shadow. When they recalled that exhilarating hike skillfully navigated on the rocks across the racing stream and to the top of the hidden waterfalls, it would be eclipsed by the sad truth that Mom was waiting at the bottom by the edge of the water. A shadow exists over our joy.

I liked you better before the accident, before you got hurt. Gwyneth said this without a hint of anger or bitterness. Nor with malice or spite. Just simple, flinty truth. I'm not sure what in particular was mulling in that beautiful head. Perhaps she was thinking about how, prior to my injury, she would immediately unclick her seatbelt the moment the car stopped and jettison herself over the console of our green Golf. When my shoes hit the pavement, I would pause just briefly; seizing this moment, she'd fling her arms around my neck and, as I rose, encircle her itty-bitty legs around my waist. I loved, loved that little monkey on my back.

Perhaps she was remembering previous adventures, like the time when we'd gone off the trail in a nearby forest preserve. We had followed the sound of water beneath the canopy of trees. When we reached the ravine, we discovered an immense old tree that had fallen, creating a bridge across the water. We considered this a personal, secret invitation and deliberated only for a few moments before we decided to lower ourselves onto the bark.

William was the first to advance upon the massive fallen tree, with John close behind, then Gwyneth and me. Gwyneth reached her arms in the air and held my hands—together we navigated our way, careful step after careful step, water rushing beneath our feet. William, like a sure-footed squirrel, easily scampered across the rounded log before he hopped to dry land, followed by his dad. Gwyneth and I, more like a pair of cats—careful, deliberate, and strongly averse to getting wet—hesitated a few times, told each other that forward was the only option, and with hearts beating a little more noticeably, jumped to safety.

Then we heard a sound coming from above us. The sound of clapping. Unbeknownst to us, an adorable elderly couple had been watching from the wooden bridge located above our heads. "Well done. Good for you!" they cheered. "We were worried for a second there. Nicely done!" The encouragement poured into our hearts caused my kids to walk a little taller for the rest of the day.

Perhaps my daughter was musing over the time when we'd been caught in a torrential downpour at a nearby park. We had only been at the playground for about ten minutes when the sky went eerily black. Before we could even get the words *It looks like rain* out of our mouths, the sky began to dump not drops but buckets of water. "Run!" someone hollered. As fast as our legs would carry us, we fled to the car—with some laughing, some howling—all the while being chased by the Texas-sized storm. By the time we reached the car, it looked as if we'd been swimming in Lake Michigan—in our clothes. Wet faces. Dripping hair. *Every* article of clothing waterlogged. Peeling those wet garments from our chilled bodies was an event in hilarity.

Perhaps now Gwyneth was thinking about little ways she needed help, ways that I could no longer be of use . . . buttons, braids, and tights. Maybe she was simply thinking about the sheer amount of time lost. Time in the park traded for time at therapy. Bike rides and games of chase usurped by hours of rehabilitation.

But make no mistake. Her suffering did not blind her to

the heavenly and holy. Quite the contrary. Gwyneth's eyes were opened to the miraculous. Her good Father in heaven was taking her by the hand and leading her into a deep faith in His Son Jesus Christ by the power of His Spirit.

Gwyneth looks back on this time with wonder and gratitude; for this is the time in her life when Jesus befriended her, becoming a balm to her open wound. This was the time when her Savior heard the prayers of a wee little girl in distress and answered the plea of her heart. Gwyneth met Jesus in the fire, the crucible, and marveled at His refining work. She had overheard doctors tell her dad that her mom would never get out of bed, that her mom would need long-term care. But in those grim days Gwyneth met the Great Physician.

When doctors were at their end, God was beginning. He breathed solace over Gwyneth's diminutive frame. She climbed into His mighty hand, curled up, and found rest; and she entrusted her mom to the same mighty grip.

30

*My child, the troubles and temptations of your life are
beginning and may be many, but you can overcome and outlive
them all if you learn to feel the strength and tenderness of your
Heavenly Father as you do that of your earthly one. The more
you love and trust Him, the nearer you will feel to Him, and
the less you will depend on human power and wisdom. His love
and care never tire or change, can never be taken from you,
but may become the source of lifelong peace, happiness,
and strength. Believe this heartily, and go to God with all
your little cares, and hopes, and sins, and sorrows, as freely
and confidingly as you come to your mother.*

—Louisa May Alcott, *Little Women*

William took a different route than his little sister.
Initially, my firstborn tried to be the best possible
son he could be. He would arrive at the hospital with a
smile and words of encouragement. If ever I was struggling,
William was quick to cheer, "Mom, you're doing great." His
bright countenance emboldened me to persevere.

But my dear sweet William could not hold up under the pressure. At the moment of my injury, life for William—and everyone else for that matter—had been completely altered. Prior to my fall, "the boys" would read together in William's bed every night. William had—and still has—a voracious love for books. I think both Will and his dad would say this was their favorite time of the day. Though John was also writing his dissertation, working hard to complete his PhD, the time spent with his yellow-haired, blue-eyed inquisitive son each evening was more precious and significant than anything else. The injury necessarily put an end to this sweet time.

Exhausted with paperwork, the task of caring for our two little ones, the demands of daily life, let alone the emotional strain of having a paralyzed wife in the hospital, John's time was devoured with things far less lovely than time with his son.

Our rented duplex was jammed with family visiting mostly from the east side of Michigan. At first, this seemed like a fun adventure. William loves, loves our families. And despite the circumstances, it was exciting to have time with the family that we weren't able to see as often as we'd like. Family took them to the sand dunes and to unexplored parks, and indulged their sweet tooths.

But the loss of our nuclear family of four was felt by William. His mom was living in a hospital miles away. The simple rhythm of our family life—breakfast, school, playing in the backyard with Gwyneth, the four of us sharing dinner in the kitchen together, more time outside, culminating with a bedtime story—had been lost. With tears streaming down his face, William cried with his daddy on our back deck one evening and told him that he wanted everyone to go home. He wanted his mom back. He wanted life to be as it was.

About eight months after my fracture, William fractured. Gwyneth, John, and I crowded into his bottom bunk bed with him one evening, and we sobbed together. He told us he felt far from God.

A few more months passed and with them came new upheaval. First, we moved from Michigan to Illinois for a teaching post for John. One year after my injury, we said goodbye to friends, William's school, and a church that loved us so well. William struggled against the uncertainties of our life. Where would we live? We were concerned our nature-loving boy would wither under city life, though Chicagoland was vast and offered parks and outdoor activities. Where would he go to school? What about friends? Church?

House-hunting was an overwhelming endeavor for everyone. Our crowded Volkswagen Golf made the trek back and forth between Michigan and Illinois several times before we settled on a rental in Glen Ellyn, a quaint town west of Chicago. This did not, however, remove the stress weighing on the shoulders of our son, because we were still not really settled. The next year we found a home in the neighboring town of Wheaton. Though it was only a few short miles away, it meant he would start fourth grade in another new school. Yet another new start. New friends. New teachers.

For William, it was a time of darkness and desolation. A time of great oppression. Pain drove him from his heavenly Father and therefore from everyone in our family. Like a cloud, he drifted from us. I felt like we were losing our son. It wasn't until we began attending a new church, our current church home, that the balm of the Holy Spirit came to bear on William's fragmented heart.

During our church's one hundred days of unceasing prayer, William wrote on a small note card, *Pray that I will want to be a Christian.* He hung it on the string among the other prayer requests in the cozy chapel adjoined to the sanctuary. Whenever it was my hour to pray, I would find William's card and move it to a spot where I thought others would see it and pray for him. My heart ached for my son. On two occasions over the next year, my heavenly Father soothed my crazed heart: *I have William*, He comforted.

Slowly but surely the poison of doubt and anxiety was extracted from William's heart. He began to carry his hopes and sins and sorrows to his heavenly Father. The small child who once told his daddy that when he grew up he wanted to sit on the porch with him, drink lemonade, and talk about Martin Luther returned to us, and was now becoming a young man. Almost six years following my injury, William, age thirteen, was confirmed in his Christian faith. Tears streamed down my face as I watched him kneel before our bishop who prayed for him by name. William, a son of God, never to be forsaken.

William, who has known great sadness but also the beautiful grace of God.

31

The most poetical thing in the world is not being sick.

—G. K. Chesterton, *The Man Who Was Thursday:*
A Nightmare

At some point in our lives, perhaps increasingly so when plunged into the darkness that often accompanies personal pain and loss, we are buffeted by the "why" of suffering. And what compounds our confusion, I believe, is the tendency to call good, or poetical if you will, that which is most definitely *not* good.

Chesterton's story begins with a confrontation between two self-proclaimed poets. One believes that poetry is synonymous with anarchy—rebellion, bombing, revolts. The other poet argues the opposite. Poetry, he contends, is defined by law, order—when things go as they should. He argues that when one is sick, his stomach is in revolt. And I think we can all agree that there's nothing poetical about that!

Prior to my injury, I worked at a conference where one of the speakers repeatedly told the thousands of women in the audience that we should thank God for virtually everything—all our trials and tribulations, including the vile things that befall us east of Eden. Similarly, I read a popular book post-injury implying that *everything* in our lives was a gift for which we should give thanks. And while this book opened my eyes to the myriad lovely details overlooked in our daily lives—church bells, train whistles, bubbles in the sink—I was perplexed at the suggestion that *all* is thanksgiving, *all* is grace. Were these super-spiritual people? Saints with whom I could not relate?

The apostle Paul, himself no stranger to trials and suffering, wrote to the church in Thessalonica, "Rejoice always, pray without ceasing, give thanks in all circumstances; for this is the will of God in Christ Jesus for you" (1 Thess. 5:16–18). Dear friends, a two-letter preposition in this phrase is ever so important. Through this letter of Paul, God exhorts us to give thanks *in* all circumstances, which is strikingly different than giving thanks *for* all circumstances. The former focuses our gaze on the One who is with us in our suffering; the latter focuses on the adversity itself! The former encourages us to look beyond our suffering, precisely to find amid our suffering the One who is just and merciful; the latter, conversely, asks us to call benevolent that which is malevolent.

I believe the common but misguided line of thinking goes something like this: *Because God is over all things, and He uses trials to bring us closer to Him, then trials are inherently good.* A deepening relationship with Jesus is the need and desire of every Christian soul. But does it always follow that the hardships themselves are good? Or is it that the beneficent Father is sometimes seen most clearly in times of tribulation, that by His supreme power He is able to bring good from that which is not, to bring redemption amid and out of difficult, dire, even diabolical situations?

We must be careful not to make the pastorally cruel mistake of calling good what God does not call good. Cancer. Tsunamis. Abuse. Broken relationships. Car accidents. Autism. Famine. And falls on the playground that leave one paralyzed. Not good. Jesus Christ in the midst of our suffering? Ah, yes, He is the comfort of the broken soul. It is as our dear little rat friend Roscuro discovered earlier: suffering is not the answer, light is the answer. I am not thankful for cancer; cancer is darkness and death. But I am thankful for Jesus Christ, who is light and life, who is present with the person vomiting hourly and watching her hair fall out in chunks. I cannot give thanks for abuse inflicted upon the child, but I can praise the One who is Father to the fatherless, who is able to mend the wounded soul.

In *Crime and Punishment*, Fyodor Dostoyevsky writes, "The darker the night, the brighter the stars; the deeper the grief, the closer is God!" Jesus Christ is the bright and beautiful star, shining in the darkness.

Consider the story of Joseph. For twenty shekels of silver, Joseph's brothers, sick with jealousy, sold him into slavery. How much would you have to hate your brother to barter for his life, then turn your back on his contorted, anguished face, ignoring his desperate pleas as you walk away, coins weighing in your pocket? And as a parent, how much would we grieve to find that the child we were raising to love and fear God, the same child who laughed with and chased his brothers and sisters, betrayed his own sibling?

As if this isn't bad enough, our hearts break over the rocks of Joseph's life once again when we enter the next chapter of his swelling tribulation. Joseph is falsely accused of attempted rape by the wife of his Egyptian master and sentenced to a life lived in the shadow, a life within the belly of a dungeon. For the next several years, his life is devoid of sunlight; he breathes the shame and weight of this perfidy.

The course of his story, however, twists when Pharaoh is awakened by a disturbing dream and someone remembers that Joseph can interpret dreams. The pale prisoner is summoned, brought into the blinding light. With freshly shaven skin, he, by God's grace, explains the meaning of Pharaoh's night terrors (warning of a time of devastating famine following a season of abundance) and is subsequently promoted to second-in-command over all the Egyptians. His chief task is to put in place a system to stockpile grain in order to prevent future mass starvation.

I wonder how long it took for Joseph's eyes to adjust to the light—the brilliance of God's beautiful plan.

Years later, the famine foretold by Joseph forces his brothers to travel to Egypt in search of grain, and we see him face-to-face with his guilty, flesh-and-blood traitors (whom he immediately identifies though they fail to recognize him). In perhaps one of the most heart-wrenching scenes in Scripture, we are invited to enter the private anguish of Joseph. The shame and loss of years set in motion by the lies and betrayal of his brothers, forgoing the power to vindicate himself, culminate in sobs as he reveals himself and rescues the brothers who tricked and tortured him. The oft-quoted words from this story are, "As for you, you meant evil against me, but God meant it for good" (Gen. 50:20). What does he mean?

Before succumbing to cancer at the age of fifty-two, Harvard law scholar of criminal justice William J. Stuntz commented on this verse, "That doesn't mean that slavery and unjust imprisonment *are* good; rather, the point is that they *produced* good, and the good they produced was larger than the wickedness that was visited upon Joseph."[16]

Make no mistake, God calls the betrayal of Joseph's brothers "evil." God, however, is good. And not only is He good, He is powerful. He takes the evil meant to humiliate and vanquish and turns it on its head. He flings it into the face of the Enemy: *You sent Joseph to die while I sent him ahead to save.* Joseph is neither blind to the evil he suffered nor to the beauty God wrought. He concludes the above verse, "to bring it about that many people should be kept alive, as they are today" (Gen. 50:20). If you start at the beginning of this story you will see a continuing thread. In the midst of trickery, trafficking, injustice, falsehood, and imprisonment, beautiful truth is stitched through—Joseph has been hemmed in by the presence of the Lord. The Lord was abiding when Joseph was a slave:

> The LORD was with Joseph so that he prospered, and he lived in the house of his Egyptian master. When his master saw that the LORD was with him and that the LORD gave him success in everything he did, Joseph found favor in his eyes and became his attendant. Potiphar put him in charge of his household, and he entrusted to his care everything he owned. (Gen. 39:2–4 NIV)

And again, the Lord was abiding when Joseph was in the dungeon: "The LORD was with him; he showed him kindness and granted him favor in the eyes of the prison warden" (v. 21 NIV). And in two separate instances, we see that God gives Joseph the ability to interpret dreams.

Joseph is not forsaken. The trials of Joseph are staggering. *But the trials are not the focal point in this narrative.* Our hearts are strengthened by the blessed truth that the kindness and wisdom of our heavenly Father is ever present on the blackest of nights, indeed in the darkest seasons of our life. For Him, we give thanks. G. K. Chesterton writes in his tale *The Man Who Was Thursday,* published in 1908:

> Shall I tell you the secret of the whole world? It is that we have only known the back of the world. We see

everything from behind, and it looks brutal. That is not a tree, but the back of a tree. That is not a cloud, but the back of a cloud. Cannot you see that everything is stooping and hiding a face? If we could only get round in front.

Indeed, if we could only get round in front of our trials to see the face of Jesus. He is our gift and blessing in the dungeon of suffering. If we focus on the trial, we will plunge either into despair or denial. If our gaze is only ever forward searching, wondering, *What good thing will come of this?* we are likely to miss *Him. He* is our present goodness and treasure.

Now what of the old rugged cross, you might ask? What of this bloody tool of torture of which we often sing? Death on a cross is not good. Jesus Himself began to sweat blood as He pondered this impending death, so let us avoid any undue sanitization of His execution.

Jesus hangs on the splintering wood, spikes in His wrists and through His feet; His head drips blood from the thorns pressed into His skull; the open lashes in His back stick to the timber; He's covered in spit; purple bruises swell from the fresh beating He's received; He's bloody, and likely naked.

With every passing minute, His body becomes heavier, pulling at the joints in His shoulders, enlarging His wounds. Upon His brow, the sun beats. His parched tongue fills His mouth. It is on this wood that Jesus became a curse. He bears and bears away the full weight of our sin and, as a result, the full wrath of God. For the first time ever, He experiences the rejection of His Father.

So what, might you ask, then makes Good Friday "good"? The corruption and treachery? The agony and angst? An innocent man bludgeoned and beaten? The Friday Jesus was condemned to the gruesome death of hanging on a cross was a day of great evil, the greatest day of evil.

But this is not the whole story of the cross. The apostle Paul proclaims to the church at Corinth, "For the word of the cross is folly to those who are perishing, but to us who are being saved it is the power of God" (1 Cor. 1:18). What does he mean? I could not begin to say this better than Charles Spurgeon.

> God must make bare His arm and bathe His sword in heaven to destroy sin wherever it is found, for He smites it even when it is imputed to His only Son! The cross thunders more terribly than Sinai, itself, against human sin! . . . Let the cross speak again and what does it say with even a louder voice? God loves men and delights in mercy! Though He loves righteousness and hates wickedness, yet He loves the sons of men so much so that He gives His only-begotten to die that sinners may live! What more could God have done to prove His love to mankind? "God commends His love to us in that, while we were yet sinners, Christ died for us." The love within that glorious deed needs

no telling, it tells itself! God had but one Son, one with Himself by mystic union and He sent Him here below to take our nature, that, being found in fashion as a man, He might die on our behalf—made *sin* for us that we might be made the *righteousness* of God in Him! "God so loved the world, that He gave His only begotten Son, that whoever believes in Him might not perish, but have everlasting life." The word of the cross is, "God is Love." He wills not the death of the sinner, but that he turn unto Him and live![17]

The cross is a vehicle of cruelty, torture, and death. But if we get round the front of the cross, we will see *Someone.* God, in His wisdom, love, and power, brought healing and forgiveness through the perfect life and bloody death of His most precious Son. The author to the Hebrews counsels, "Let us throw off everything that hinders and the sin that so easily entangles. And let us run with perseverance the race marked out for us, fixing *our eyes on Jesus*, the pioneer and perfecter of faith. For the joy set before him he endured the cross, scorning its shame, and sat down at the right hand of the throne of God. *Consider him* who endured such opposition from sinners, so that you will not grow weary and lose heart" (Heb. 12:1–3 NIV, emphasis added).

On Good Friday at my home church, we traditionally lay a massive cross of timber on the floor at the front of the sanctuary. We come and kneel at the cross, acknowledging our sin and bringing our burdens to Jesus. At the cross, Jesus Christ meets us in our sin and suffering. Here we see the profound and deep love of God for us. We see once again how God curbs the evil intention of the Enemy and forces defeat down his throat. Here we enter into true poetry, the life, the death, and the resurrection of Jesus Christ. Jesus has borne our pain so that we might be restored and re-created body and soul. We are united with Him in body and spirit; thus, we are reunited with the Father, becoming sons and daughters of the One true God.

PART FIVE

the way home

32

*"I was the lion who forced you to join with Aravis. I was the
cat who comforted you among the houses of the dead. I was
the lion who drove the jackals from you as you slept. I was the
lion who gave the Horses the new strength of fear for the
last mile so that you should reach King Lune in time. And I
was the lion you do not remember who pushed the boat in
which you lay, a child near death, so that it came to shore
where a man sat, wakeful at midnight, to receive you."*

—C. S. Lewis, *The Horse and His Boy*

One year after my injury, we said goodbye to Grand
Rapids—a place forever forged on our hearts. The
goodbye was bittersweet, as are most goodbyes. We had
been loved profoundly during our last year in Michigan.
But the farewell was also sweet as we were embarking on a
new adventure, John having received a teaching post in the
theology department at Moody Bible Institute in Chicago.

About a half hour after arriving at the house we were
renting just west of the city, Gwyneth, then five, asked her

daddy if he would write down our new address and phone number. Why? She informed him that she wanted to knock on some neighborhood doors, ask if any kids lived there, and if so, explain that she was new in town, and looking for new friends. Gwyneth has always been our socially brave girl.

So imagine our surprise when after only a few months of kindergarten she began to tell us she didn't want to go to school. This was the same girl who had lamented the previous year that she was too young to stay in school for a full day. What was the problem? Gwyneth already had several friends in her new school and was having no trouble academically. But she persisted to ask if she didn't have to go to school. So one night when tucking her into bed, I asked again: "Why?" She thought for a moment and then said something simple, yet profound: "My new teacher doesn't know me."

This certainly wasn't the case for prekindergarten. Gwyneth started pre-K with Mrs. Schumaker, a teacher who'd already known her three of the four years of her life (William also had Mrs. Schumaker for pre-K). In fact, Pam Schumaker is a dear friend of mine. She was with Gwyneth in the hospital the night of my surgery and was a tremendous support after my injury. So when Gwyneth started school with Mrs. Shumaker the year after I got hurt, no introductions were necessary. But this year she had to introduce herself to her new teacher. "Mom," she said, "I had tears in my eyes."

Do we not all struggle with doubt, disbelieving that we are seen, loved, known? When William was only three, he and I left his dad in Toronto while we visited our family in east Michigan. One day Will called his daddy only to hear the beep of the answering machine. "Daddy, Daddy," he said quietly. "Are you there? Do you remember me?" We kept that message, re-listening to it for months. It made our hearts smile and break all at the same time.

How precious it is to be known and loved—to be embraced by someone who knows your pain, sensitivities, joys, strengths, weaknesses, and fears. Our hearts long to be known. And not just to be known, but to be loved—in spite of ourselves. For an honest peek into our hearts reveals darkness, our propensities to selfishness, pride, ingratitude, apathy, greed, anxiety, and doubt. Victor Hugo communicated this brilliantly when he said, "Life's great happiness is to be convinced we are loved."

I have never been a fan of crowds. For in the crowd, you can get lost. You're unknown, unseen, and unimportant. Your existence is inconsequential. But when Jesus is thronged among the masses in Luke 8, the effect is surprising. Here's how I envision the scene.

The people press in and emit all the telltale smells of a crowd. Many are elbowing their way, jockeying to get closer, to catch a glimpse of the man behind the stories. With a tremulous heart, the synagogue ruler Jairus walks just ahead of Jesus.

Stomach churning, Jairus's thoughts are of his only daughter, the brightness of his eyes and just twelve years old, on her death bed. Jesus is his one hope, his last hope.

As Jesus follows the shaken father, a woman is mustering the courage to come near to Him—but not too near. The hope that she buried so long ago—beneath the pain, beneath the blood, covered with the exasperated, sometimes condescending looks of physicians and their words "nothing else can be done"—within this graveyard of suffering and isolation, hope begins to tap. It began lightly, perhaps when she first heard the name *Jesus*. But the tapping increased when she heard murmurings of healing, authority, real power. *Could it be? Could He be?*

The closer she gets, the more intensely hope raps, until it's beating like a drum threatening to betray her. Heart palpitating, she inches forward. Her eyes are cast upon the ground, upon the moving sandaled feet, dust, and flowing garments. She reaches for Jesus and allows her fingertips to brush the fringe of His cloak. And in that moment, she knows. I imagine her stopping in place, allowing the crowd to continue around her. Oh Lord, all the pain, the years and years of pain and separation, twelve years of compounded disappointment, of persevering in the midst of fatigue, have all been bound up in this moment.

She *feels* again. She'd almost forgotten what it felt like to be normal, to feel normally, unburdened. And while basking in this surreal, sublime moment she realizes that the crowd has stopped moving. A bond has been established between Jesus and this dear soul, and He doesn't want her to miss it. He doesn't want her to slip away without knowing that He has seen her in her pain; she is no longer hidden.

She falls at the feet of her healer, trembling like a thief caught in the act. But none take from Jesus what He does not freely, even gladly, give. Jesus has restored the body of this woman and her life. She hears the kindness in His voice as He calls her "Daughter." In this moment, despite the spying crowd and the distraught father Jairus, Jesus is fully present with this woman. All the suffering she has experienced at the hands of other doctors has been healed by the true physician. "Daughter, your faith has made you well; go in peace." (See Luke 8:40–48)

The event with Gwyneth happened prior to the Advent season, and I was struck by the truth that our hearts' longing to be known is answered in that thrill of hope come to us in the manger. Jesus Christ *knows*. He knows what it's like to be among a crowd of people, but to be known by none of them. He knows exhaustion, suffering, betrayal, rejection, and loneliness. Dear reader, He knows. And perhaps a truth even more precious, He knows us intimately.

O LORD, you have searched me and known me!
You know when I sit down and when I rise up;
you discern my thoughts from afar.
You search out my path and my lying down
and are acquainted with all my ways.
Even before a word is on my tongue,
behold, O LORD, you know it altogether.
You hem me in, behind and before,
and lay your hand upon me. (Psalm 139:1–5)

33

"Child," said the Lion, *"I am telling you your story, not hers. No one is told any story but their own."*

—C. S. Lewis, *The Horse and His Boy*

The ways of our heavenly Father are mysterious. I do not know why my young twenty-one-year-old hospital roommate who fell from a zip line did not heal. One minute the college-aged senior was suspended high in the air, her long hair flowing as she cascaded along her family's new zip-wired ride; the next minute, with a snap, she was plummeting rapidly downward, only stopping when her slight body collided with the ground.

She arrived at the hospital a few weeks after I did. The healthy young student thought she would walk out of the hospital soon after she arrived, and her doctors did not seem to discourage this hope. She had a lower back injury that left her with complete control of her upper body and movement in her lower extremities. With a little therapy, it seemed, she would be mobile, walking, dancing, climbing. But she made little progress over the few short weeks she was at the hospital. She could sometimes walk, though crudely and awkwardly with the aid of two canes, but her physicians had little confidence in her balance, and she went home in a wheelchair.

I do not know why none of my tetraplegic companions walked out of the hospital. Not even the friend I'd first watched in awe taking steps in the pool. After a full year of inpatient therapy, he went home in a wheelchair. I watched the agonized face of my Harley-Davidson friend struggle to do anything with his hands. Once an independent spirit, an adventurous risk-taker, now a vulnerable soul needing full-time care and assistance with dressing, eating, all things having to do with the bathroom. I felt sorrow for the man who'd fallen down his basement steps, broken his neck, and now filled the air with anger and expletives. He too left the hospital in a wheelchair.

I did not ask the Lord, "Why *me*?" when I got hurt. We all have stories of suffering. In the twelve years John and I had been married, we had known trial and tragedy: financial hardship, sizeable rats in our Dallas apartment, the malfunctioning heart of our preborn son William, four major moves, further financial stress, and about a year before my injury, under the weight of his doctoral program, John brooked a scary bout of extreme mental and emotional fatigue. We have known fear that binds, sorrow so full it chokes, and circumstances that struck us like an axe—one fell swoop leveling us to the ground.

Nevertheless, we were not in the habit of asking, "Why did this happen to us? Why *me*? Why did *I* get hurt?" Rarely, if ever, does anyone receive an answer to the "why" question. And a close reading of Scripture reveals that "Why?" isn't even the question we should be asking. Consider this story from the apostle John's gospel:

As he passed by, he saw a man blind from birth. And his disciples asked him, "Rabbi, who sinned, this man or his parents, that he was born blind?" Jesus answered, "It was not that this man sinned, or his parents, but that the works of God might be displayed in him." (John 9:1–3)

The disciples presented the same type of question that plagues us today. Why did this happen? Why is this man blind? And who is to blame? The blind man? His parents? God? There is an accusing tone, a finger-wagging betrayed in these questions, is there not? We know that sin and suffering are intertwined. This is evident throughout Scripture. But what is the cause of or reason for the specific suffering in our own lives?

Pastor and theologian Helmut Thielicke referred to this very passage of John when he preached amid the ruin and rubble of Germany during World War II:

Do we not all know this troublesome questioner within us who in contempt or despair, in sorrow or accusation constantly asks, "Why?" This little word "why" is no torrent of speech. It is only a drop of three letters. Yet it can cause mortal injury to our souls.[18]

Who does not know the despair that chaperones the question *Why?* Why did the dreams I had for my child never come to fruition? Why, after countless hours of sleep deprivation and financial sacrifice, did my child forsake and reject me? Why did all my hard work and effort result in a hostile job environment with seeming pointlessness while so many others seem to flourish happily? Why is disease, sickness, and violence stealing so many lives this and every passing day? Why did this evil thing happen?

But if "Why?" is not the right question, what question should, *must* we ask? To the broken and battered people who survived the air raid, Thielicke continued:

There is thus manifested a tremendous liberation, which Jesus brings to us in our need and in our bitter thoughts. For He teaches us to put our question in a way which is meaningful. He tells us that we should not ask "Why?" but "To what end?" In thus fashioning the question Jesus is a true Pastor. For when we understand the change, we are no longer choked with terror.

We can breathe again. We can cry and not be weary. We can live by the profound peace in our hearts.[19]

"Why?" turns us inward, and the more inwardly we gaze, the deeper and darker is our despair. Stuffing ourselves with self, we are ushered into a corridor of self-pity with its close companions, misery and bitterness. The question "To what end?", however, turns our hearts back to our kindhearted Father who bids us come, to trust in Him, to rest in His promise that though sadness and grief, pain and hardship are ever with us now, He sees and is all the time working powerfully toward ends that are good, ends that are more beautiful and impossible than we could ever imagine.

Many have braved *far* greater heartache than my family. Some have endured less. In the rehabilitation hospital, I was not bowed down so much by the question of why *I* got hurt, but I couldn't help but wonder why *I* was being healed. Injured patients at the hospital watched my progress, and as they did, hope stirred in their hearts. But some despaired. I was getting better and they were not.

I am humbled as I think about what my life would look like apart from the healing that has occurred. I am humbled because I know other families also prayed that their loved ones would get better only to experience the silence of God. I will not presume, in such cases, to know the inner thoughts or plans of our triune God. Yet I trust that His ends are good. I am tremendously blessed by brothers and sisters in Christ who continue to cling to Jesus even when—especially when—the pain and suffering is nearly too much to bear.

Thielicke says that God is a God of ends. The blind man is blind so that the works of God might be displayed in him. Rather than take the position of accuser, which leads us to discouragement and despair, we must set our eyes on Jesus and the ends for which He calls us.

> Everything changes under our hands if with our hand in the hand of our Lord we are ready to march forward to the great ends of God. Our conscience is stained and we are guilty. But being in the hand of Jesus, we may ask with fear and trembling, "To what end?" and we may receive the answer of Paul: In order that grace may be mightier, the cross greater, and the Lord dearer to us.[20]

34

Adventures are never fun while you're having them.

—C. S. Lewis, *The Voyage of the Dawn Treader*

In the Clark home, we firmly believe days that end by crawling into bed with a book are better than days that do not. We *all* love a good story.

Over the years, we've read books together as a family. William and Gwyneth, much to their parents' envy, have stolen away and read entire books in a day. And as I reflect, I realize some of our most cherished moments as parents have been through shared stories. We love to crowd into the story, as there is something thrilling about walking alongside a character we've befriended. We agonize. We hope. We laugh and cry (well, I do the lion's share of the crying). In a sense, we rejoice and suffer right along with the characters.

The adventure, however, isn't nearly as fun when you, yourself, are in the middle of it. I have been encouraged again and again to share my story. But, in truth, I'm not always eager to share. To be sure, there are moments when I just know I *must* tell the story, but often I am hesitant.

The story is big. A few short sentences won't do it justice.

The story is bold. I'm a healed quadriplegic.

In short, I'm a miracle.

I stutter over actually uttering those words aloud. They seem boastful, perhaps a bit braggadocious. And I know myself well enough to be ever cognizant of my innumerable edges and flaws.

The story is beautiful, yet it is also beastly. I'm never quite sure where to cut off the story. Do I end on a high "I was healed!" note, or do I divulge my ongoing pain and limitations?

I'm enjoying a cup of coffee at my dear friend's home, seated among the women from our Bible study. The group leader suggests we share with one another something about ourselves that others might not know.

I'm quiet. I listen. After almost everyone has shared, two women who know my story look at me and bid, "Kate, share the story. Will you, please?"

I'm happy to share an abridged version of the horrible, wonderful story. Looks of bewilderment and awe follow. Heads nod after someone utters, "That's amazing!" We move on to the next woman who says what I expect, "I don't have anything to share after that." I hate when the story severs the discussion. I hate when the story culminates in a comparison of cross bearing and, as a result, a chasm between us.

Much to my dismay, my story is sometimes the tale that

trumps other stories. After I share, no one ever responds, "Oh my, that very thing happened to me. I too was paralyzed, diagnosed a quadriplegic, and now I can walk."

One thing, however, I experienced time and time again during my days in the hospital is the reality that we *all* have stories—and none of them are devoid of hardship or suffering. The nurse who desperately wanted a baby but could not conceive. The nurse whose brother died in a drunk driving accident. The nurse whose child was autistic. The nursing assistant with the troubled marriage. As we became friends, each of these hospital staffers shared with me the heavy stones weighing on their hearts. I did not think, *What are you complaining about? At least you have your health. At least you have use of your hands. You can walk.* I was, instead, honored and blessed. Here were women sharing in my suffering. I was grateful they allowed me to share in theirs.

My pastor says that stories change the world. I commit my story to writing with the hope that Jesus will be glorified, and in doing so, hearts will indeed be restored. I trust that someday we will cast our glances back over the adventures of our lives and take pleasure in the holy history authored by our heavenly Father—tales fraught with pain but cleverly spun into truth, beauty, hope, love, and victory.

Those who are hidden in Jesus, though we suffer, will discover a more beautiful ending—or really should I say beginning—than we ever could imagine. Book One of our lives is the tale of rebellion, loss, suffering, and redemption.

Book Two is a perfectly new tale—the living out of our redeemed lives, where, sin being wholly rooted from our hearts, minds, and souls, reigns no longer and holiness governs, where joy is written upon every page.

35

"I don't like anything here at all," said Frodo, "step or stone,
breath or bone. Earth, air and water all seem accursed.
But so our path is laid."
"Yes, that's so," said Sam, "And we shouldn't be here
at all, if we'd known more about it before we started. But I
suppose it's often that way . . . I wonder what sort of a tale
we've fallen into?"
"I wonder," said Frodo, "but I don't know. And that's the way of
a real tale. Take any one that you're fond of. You may know, or
guess, what kind of a tale it is, happy-ending or sad-ending, but
the people in it don't know. And you don't want them to."

—J. R. R. Tolkien, *The Two Towers*

It is a great mercy of God that we cannot see the future.
For scarcely do I think we could get out of bed if we knew
the perils and sadness that is to come. When Mary held
her baby close to her breast and pondered the tiny fingers
wrapped around her finger, little did she know the hard story
that had already been written. Surely as a mother, she held

buoyant, bright dreams for her child. And no doubt she
replayed the words of the angel again and again in her heart:

Do not be afraid, Mary . . . you will conceive in your
womb and bear a son, and you shall call his name Jesus.
He will be great and will be called the Son of the Most
High. And the Lord God will give to him the throne
of his father David, and he will reign over the house of
Jacob forever, and of his kingdom there will be no end.
(Luke 1:30–33)

She must have joyously anticipated what it would look
like for her son to be "great." Did she imagine him inheriting
the throne and reigning? And what must Mary and Joseph
have thought when they took the infant Jesus to the temple
and the aged man Simeon blessed God, saying that now that
he had seen His salvation, he was ready to die. Surely Mary
and Joseph left asking each other what Simeon meant when
he said that their child would be appointed for the fall and
rise of many in Israel (see Luke 2:29–34). Oh what hope
they must have carried within them for this child who was
clearly set apart, the testified "salvation" of God.

And oh the rupturing of Mary's heart, the desolation
she must have felt as she stood at the foot of the execution
place and craned her neck upward to see her son hanging
on two planks of timber, naked, shameful, pierced, bloody,
broken—the very life she had carried and nurtured in her

womb, dying, draining out before her. How her mother's heart must have crumbled as she listened to the crowd, full of scorn and contempt for her child. This was not how it was supposed to end. What about the promises, the bright future proclaimed by the angel?

How many a mother and father have looked on a casket holding their child and grieved the once bright future they'd envisioned now as dead as the body before them? How many parents, brothers, sisters, husbands, wives, and friends have thought, dear God, this is not how it was supposed to end. I cannot help but think that when my parents saw me lying in bed paralyzed their hearts must have thought back to the vibrant girl who loved music and dancing and life. And they must have grieved in a way that only parents grieve.

I cannot help but think that my husband must have been drawn back to that hot, sunny day in July when in a garden of flowers and green we promised to love each other, no matter what. It must have seemed like a bold, perhaps naïve, thing to do now that he was attempting to comprehend life with a woman utterly dependent on him and two children who would need him more than ever. And William and Gwyneth —what thoughts must have been running wild in their heads. *Will we always have to feed Mom? Will she never run or play or swing with us again? What about family trips? Will we take them? And what will that look like?*

I don't think we're wired to handle the whole story at once. Eve, in the garden, wanted to know all the things that

God knew. The Enemy suggested to her that God did not want to share, that God was stingy—a hoarder who somehow felt threatened by the knowledge Eve would gain from disobeying His instruction not to eat from the tree in the middle of the garden.

But Eve failed to comprehend that, in His love, God was protecting her, the daughter He loved, from the knowledge of evil, for He knew that once she tasted sin, her heart and all hearts after her would break. And that, of course, is what happened. No life since has been lived without lies, disease, fear, sorrow, loneliness, meanness, grief, or loss.

And if we knew the full onslaught of evil that would befall our lives, the whole of our story relayed in one story-time session, we'd have a hard time stepping into the sunlight. No mother holds her son and imagines that someday his little body will get cancer, or that he will suffer a bitter divorce, or become sick with depression. No father holds his baby girl and wonders if someday she will be the victim of terrible abuse, or be crippled with anxiety, or give herself over to a life of drugs or alcohol. It is inconceivable for a parent to imagine these possibilities, sometimes realities, of life. Instead, we dream. We dream for our children. We nourish and nurture hope, not only for our own lives but for the lives of those we love.

In God's vast mercy, we live the stories of our lives one page at a time. For sometimes a chapter so painful will come, we are tempted to lament that we'd even started the story.

But when we bear the sorrow, one sorrow at a time, honestly and with a measure of rebellious hope, instead of becoming paralyzed or mending crooked, we come through with a quiet strength, a peculiar beauty that only sorrow can forge.

36

It has always seemed to me, ever since early childhood, that, amid all the commonplaces of life, I was very near to a kingdom of ideal beauty. Between it and me hung only a thin veil. I could never draw it quite aside, but sometimes a wind fluttered it and I caught a glimpse of the enchanting realm beyond—only a glimpse—but those glimpses have always made life worth while.

—L. M. Montgomery, author of *Anne of Green Gables*

Imagine going through the day wearing mittens and you will get some idea of what my current life is like. It's not that you can't get through the day, it's just challenging and annoying.

Helping your daughter pull up her tights will prove to be a frustrating experience. Braiding her hair—well, let's hope she's patient. Holding a pen, tricky. Opening a Ziploc bag—these things are hard enough to open even if you do have feeling in your fingers, so imagine trying to open them with gloves on. Tying shoes, zipping zippers, buttoning shirts, turning pages in a book, prying open Tupperware, sorting change, putting on jewelry—even if you're patient, the victories here are few and far between.

Because your hands feel as if they're asleep, you're a pro at spilling and dropping things, which you do on a regular basis. You've watched countless dishes slip from your hands and smash at your feet. Both of your favorite mugs—gifts—bear the chips and cracks of your clumsiness.

You've even dropped a teakettle of boiling water down your leg.

Your hands feel a bit like a towel caught in a door. Every time you attempt to bend them, you're impaired. But the muscle impairment and joint pain isn't confined to your hands; spasticity—a muscle control disorder—wreaks havoc throughout your hands and lower limbs. When fatigue sets in, which it does each and every night, the muscles in your legs stiffen, jerk, and spasm.

Your body has difficulty determining where it is in space (something referred to as proprioception), resulting in weekly burns, cuts, and bruises, often inflicted in the kitchen. When your child sees yet another cut, she confesses that she feels guilty that she was not home to help; had she been home, she laments, this would not have happened.

For most people, walking happens seamlessly, beautifully. But this isn't the case with you. Your right side is weaker than your left, so balance and coordination can be a problem. At times, you may appear tipsy, slightly inebriated. To be sure, you've come a long way. You started out after the accident so awkwardly, fearing you'd never attain a "normal" gait. The process has been humbling, sometimes humiliating. Yet still today, you have to think about walking. Occasionally you muse, *I wonder if this looks "normal"* or you catch a glimpse of your reflection in a window and think, *I don't recognize that stiff, uncoordinated person.*

Your right hip hikes up higher than the left. Because it feels as if someone has filled your legs with sand, each step is laborious, a challenge. Sometimes your right side simply gives way, causing you to stumble, trip, or fall at the most inopportune times. When you're fatigued, your right leg begins to drag. You can no longer run, which is particularly sad now that your son is older, for you would love to run alongside and talk and laugh and tease that boy, now a young man.

Balance, muscle issues, and proprioception combine to create the perfect storm when it comes to navigating steps. Descending stairs, a particularly dangerous endeavor, is not always successful. The worst string of falls was four within ten months, each time on the unforgiving hardwood steps in your home. I'm not sure if it's worse when it happens and you're all by yourself, or if it's more tragic when your kids actually witness the rapid wreck of back and elbows and bum colliding with the immovable planks. I think the latter, not because it's humiliating, but because you don't want to keep piling worry and sorrow onto their young hearts.

Finally, you suffer from chronic paresthesia—nerve pain, that burning pins-and-needles sensation that feels like a thousand angry bee stings, buzzing, throbbing in your hands, down your left side, and in your feet. You live daily with muscle pain that ranges from a constant dull ache to a sharp, stiff-necked fire. The medicine, which you do not like to swallow, curbs the blaze, but isn't able to eliminate it.

Every minute of every day is punctuated, capped with pain. Mornings and evenings are peak times. And though you feel like an elderly person saying it, change in temperature or the metamorphosis of the seasons affect your nerves and muscles. The Midwest winters are markedly brutal. Not only does the chill of the air lodge within your muscles, causing them to seize and stiffen, it also makes a home in all the little blood vessels of your fingers and feet, leaving your digits deathly white or purplish-blue. You spend your winter days blowing warm breath on your frigid fingers, bidding the clinging chill to flee. Warm mugs of cider and hot cocoa are welcome friends.

Then, of course, there is some residual aftermath too personal and shameful to speak about, certainly far too vulnerable to detail in a book. Some particulars, for the sake of everyone, must be safeguarded.

To your brain, not much seems to make sense still. Progress is labored and awkward. You continue to attend therapy in an ongoing effort to maintain health and physical functioning. And tucked away in a box in your basement closet is a letter from your spinal cord rehabilitation doctor indicating that your central cord syndrome/Brown-Séquard syndrome will affect you for the rest of your life, that as you age, residual deficits will become even more apparent.

Make no mistake, dear reader, I'm profoundly grateful for the healing that's taken place. I know what it feels like to lie in a bed helpless, unable to move. My kids have memories of feeding me, driving my wheelchair, and so much more. We all have a deep appreciation for the truth that we're fearfully and wonderfully made. And for that very reason, we grieve. Not as those bereft of hope, yet we grieve nonetheless. Because grief is the faithful response to loss.

I miss chasing my kids. I have this vision of childhood; it involves chasing and laughter and little bare feet running in the green grass—an image that has become one of those dreams you desperately want but cannot get back to. I miss waking up in the morning feeling robust and able-bodied. Every morning I am aroused by an alarm clock of pain, a burning and throbbing sensation in my hands, and cramping in my legs. Throughout the day, I fight back fatigue, a young woman dwelling in a body that feels old.

I miss seemingly insignificant abilities to which I once gave little thought, like how my fingers used to fly over the keys of my computer. (For a long time John and I had an ongoing, friendly feud over who was the speedier typist. This is no longer an open line of debate.)

I miss high heels and flip-flops; I lack the coordination to wear either. I deeply miss that natural rhythm and spring I once had in my step.

I miss what I have missed, like swing dancing in the downtown square of Grand Rapids. Prior to my injury, John promised to take me to the free lessons hosted once a week in the city under the evening summer sun that were then followed by a swing fest. I am lost to experiencing the reverie of flipping and spinning to the Big Band music.

I miss being adventurous with William and Gwyneth—and hope that when they are grown they will not remember all the things I could not do. Nicholas Wolterstorff, former professor at Yale University, said this about grief and loss:

> I own my grief. I do not try to put it behind me, to get over it, to forget it. I do not try to *dis*-own it. . . . That loss determines my identity; not all of my identity, but much of it. It belongs within my story. I struggle indeed to go beyond merely owning my grief toward owning it *redemptively*. But I will not and cannot disown it.[21]

Wolterstorff's words pulse in my heart. The past years have been a season of tears in the Clark home. Tears of grief for our loss, and for my pain and limitations. And also tears of joy for my amazing progress and for the sweet kindness of God. I live in the midst of this tension—gratitude and grief—every day.

I live gratefully beneath the shadow of pain and sorrow.

Perhaps the greatest irony in my story is that I have very little *normal* feeling from the neck down. And yet, though sensation is muted in my physical body, I can also say that since my injury, I *feel* more acutely than ever. William is right. After my fall, he mused, "Mom cries all the time now." Life perforates my increasingly penetrable heart in a distinctly different way. Stories of sadness, stories of triumph and joy resonate, uprooting the broken ground of my heart, releasing a torrent of sorrow, delight, wonder, and love.

I long, dear friend, for a heavenly home. A home without chronic nerve pain and muscle fatigue. A home where I don't hurt others, where I don't get hurt. I long to feel and hold William's and Gwyneth's hands in my own. Because I cannot feel their grip in mine, I often squeeze too hard, or simply feel their hands slip from my grasp. I asked Gwyneth when she was six—two years after the trauma—if it would be all right with her if we held hands for about the first fifty years we were in heaven; she thought that was a grand idea. That same year our little sage—her first grade teacher referred to her as "an old soul"—was listening to a CD of Christmas hymns for the children's church choir and said, "Divine. Mom, I don't know what that word means, but I like it. What does divine mean? I just love how it sounds."

Divine: having the nature of deity; supremely good or beautiful; magnificent[22]

Do our hearts not long for the divine? A God who is supremely good and beautiful. One who enters into our suffering lives, breathing forgiveness and hope, and the promise to make all things right, all well. Each Christmas we celebrate the child divine. The star of royal beauty bright, in whom the deepest longings of our hearts are satisfied.

We are very near, as Lucy Maud Montgomery ruminated, to a kingdom of ideal beauty. We catch glimpses of the enchanted realm encouraging our hearts to persevere. When my children were small, I would stealthily slip into their rooms in the night hours to catch a peek of them slumbering. And seeing them in their beds, I would sometimes catch my breath, caught off guard by the holiness of the moment. The beauty of their expressions, perfectly serene and at rest, caused my heart to feel as if it just might break, it was so utterly full.

In that sacred moment, I felt as if the world had for one brief moment stopped spinning—and all was good and just as it should be. Looking back, I sometimes long to return to this sublime break in time, yet we can only get back to this realm by looking forward. We hold fast to the promise that our supremely good Father will, by the power of His Spirit, bring us home to live alongside His most precious Son. Oh Lord, what a good day that will be.

37

Life is a mess and a miracle.

—Jennifer Trafton, *The Rise and Fall of Mount Majestic*

Everyone has a story, and this is mine. At least this is a few pages in my story, for we can never know the whole of one's story.

I said at the beginning of this book that my story did not have a fairy-tale ending. I am not like the lame man who Jesus told to walk, who immediately took up his mat and was fully healed. I am tempted to think that had my healing been as such, doubters—myself included—would have simply concluded that my injury was not as serious as we thought. Had I not been through hours, days, months of rehabilitation, or if I did not feel the subsequent current of burning pain in my present body, I might have thought differently about the nature of my injury or been quick to forget the massiveness of the blow.

I was raised wounded. Yet, dear reader, to say that my

story doesn't have a perfectly sublime ending isn't quite true. For I will not always be wounded. I will not always bear this pain, carry this sorrow.

As I mentioned, our little Clark family loves stories. We love to befriend the characters, to laugh with or cheer for them. We argue in our heads, urging, sometimes begging them to resist evil, to make the right choice, to be brave. We grieve when they are thwarted, even if it's their own fault. We join in their joy and frustrations. Most of all, we long to see the characters whom we've come to love be healed, defended, and redeemed. We love stories because deep within us they are reminiscent of another story, a true story.

Sometimes we'll be reading a book, and it will take a turn none of us had foreseen. Jesus, the God-hero, became a baby. The Son of God became *human*. This unexpected, surprise twist, I suspect, left all participants in the story awestruck. And when, as a young man, Jesus willingly went to the cross to bear and bear away our sin, well, I don't think anyone would have penned it quite like that. What kind of God becomes small, walks alongside His people, subjects Himself to betrayal, scorn, suffering, shame, and even death—another true-life literary stunner.

We are the characters who created the mess, and the triune God of the Bible responded by initiating a miracle. God came to rescue His own, a people who desired to write their own stories, stories lived apart from Him.

But a life lived apart from the One who created, knows, and

loves you—the One who rejoices in blessing and caring for you—that, dear friends, would be a tragedy of catastrophic proportion. That is not the grand finale penned by the Father. Despite the selfish, hard, bitter, apathetic hearts of His children, His love could not be thwarted. He came. He came, writing a story that would resonate deep within our hearts, a story of forgiveness and love. He came, because in Him and no other is hope, joy, and sustenance.

And when our hearts grapple with pain and darkness, we can lean into the promise that He shall come again. This is where it begins to feel a bit like a fairy tale. Someday God will put to right all that is wrong, both in the world and in our hearts. Someday He will heal our souls and bodies. Someday we will live "happily ever after." Not in the unrealistic, saccharine sense portrayed in second-rate movies or novels. But in a way that is more real and true than we could imagine. Someday we will resemble the lovely little character Polly from *The Rise and Fall of Mount Majestic*:

> Her legs gave way beneath her, and she sank to her knees. She had not imagined big enough. She had only thought about *finding* the giant. She hadn't thought about *seeing* it. She had believed in it, but she hadn't really considered it being real. She had not stopped to picture in her mind what it would be like to be here alone, looking at it—him.[23]

Someday our legs will indeed give way. We will sink and see that we had not imagined Him big enough. We had thought about finding God. We hadn't thought about actually seeing Jesus. When we do, we will find Him—nail wounds and all—more beautiful and powerful than we could have ever imagined.

We will be with Him, our Jesus.

Our bodies will breathe a sigh of relief. Sorrow will drain from the tips of our fingers.

We will tremble with joy.

And our hearts will sing a song of gladness, a song that will forever endure.

FOR REFLECTION
AND DISCUSSION

1. Have you experienced a defining event in your life that causes you to look back and say, "that was before _____" or "that happened after _____"? Did the event change you? In what way(s)? How can you see God's hand throughout the experience?

2. When someone expresses fear, sadness, loneliness, or another difficult emotion, our response is often: "Don't feel that way." Is this helpful? If not, what are better responses? Does God invite our honest thoughts and feelings? Explain your answer.

3. Rather than asking "Why?" about the difficulties that come to each life, the author quotes Helmut Thielicke, who says, "To what end?" What is the difference between the two when we contemplate suffering?

4. Kate describes two common responses to grief: to see grief as "an unwelcome, uninvited trespasser to be

shunned or dismissed;" or as "a friend, a codependent lover," something not to be shunned but "indulged at every opportunity."

Do you agree with these descriptions? When have you seen people respond in either of these ways to grief? What alternative approach, if any, does Kate recommend?

5. Kate states that not only is the Christian joined to Christ, Christians are joined to one another. Is this an aspect of Christian doctrine? If so, what Scriptures support it? How have you seen this played out?

6. Kate describes a time of darkness and desolation her son William went through. Have you experienced a similar dark time of the soul? What was it like, and how did you get through it? How might you encourage another person going through something similar?

7. Kate describes hearing a speaker say we should thank God for everything that happens to us, including terrible troubles. What does she conclude about this viewpoint? What is the difference between something *being* good and something *producing* good?

8. Gwyneth became reluctant to go to her new school because she felt her teacher didn't *know* her. When have

you felt that you have and have not been known? Kate says, "How precious it is to be known and loved—embraced by someone who knows your pain, sensitivities, joys, strengths, weaknesses, and fears." Read Psalm 139. How do you react to being known by God?

NOTES

1. C. S. Lewis, *A Grief Observed* (New York: HarperCollins, 1961, 1996), 52.

2. John Kavanaugh, *America*, vol. 173, no. 10 ()ctober 7, 1995): 23.

3. Herbert Kretzmer, "Do You Hear the People Sing?" © 1980, written for the musical Les Misérables based on Victor Hugo's book.

4. Karl Barth, *Church Dogmatics*, IV/1, ed. G. W. Bromiley and T. F. Torrance, trans. G. W. Bromiley (Peabody, MA: Hendrickson, 2010), 410.

5. Thomas F. Torrance, *The Mediation of Christ*, rev. ed. (Colorado Springs, CO: Helmers & Howard, 1992), xiv.

6. Kate DiCamillo, *The Miraculous Journey of Edward Tulane* (Cambridge, MA: Candlewick Press, 2006), 180.

7. Josiah Bell, Mat Kearney, Robert Martin, "Closer to Love," ©2009 (album City of Black & White).

8. W. H. Auden, "As I Walked Out One Evening," in *Another Time* (New York: Random House, 1940).

9. Jack Noble White, "First Song of Isaiah," The H. W. Gray Company, admin. Warner Bros. Publications U.S., Inc., 1977.

10. *Mayo Clinic Guide to Living with a Spinal Cord Injury* (New York: Demos Medical Publishing, 2009), 9.

11. Gregory of Nazianzus, "To Cledonius the Priest against Apollinarius," Letters on the Apollinarian Controversy, no. 101, in NPNF, 7:440.

12. Blaise Pascal, *Pensées*, no. 417, trans. A. J. Krailsheimer (New York: Penguin, 1995), 141.

13. Helmut Thielicke, *Out of the Depths,* trans. G. W. Bromiley (Grand Rapids: William B. Eerdmans Publishing Company, 1962), 12.

14. *The Velveteen Rabbit*, a beloved classic, was written by Margery Williams in 1922.

15. *Mayo Clinic Guide to Living with a Spinal Cord Injury*, 81–82.

16. William J. Stuntz, *Christianity Today* (August 2009).

17. "The Word of the Cross," Sermon #1611, www.spurgeongems.org, vol. 27; delivered July 31, 1881.

18. Helmut Thielicke, *Out of the Depths*, 13.

19. Ibid., 15.

20. Ibid., 19.

21. Nicholas Wolterstorff, *Lament for a Son* (Grand Rapids: Wm. B. Eerdmans Publishing Co., 1987), 5–6.

22. https://ahdictionary.com/word/search.html?q=divine.

23. Jennifer Trafton, *The Rise and Fall of Mount Majestic* (New York: Penguin, 2010), 136.

ACKNOWLEDGMENTS

It takes a village to raise a child. But I have found that we don't shed our need for the village once we're grown. We are built for community and still need that steady undergirding of encouragement and support. To that end, I joyfully give thanks to my village, the friends and family who have been my foundation, without whom this work could not have come to fruition. Thank you to my marketing and editing team, especially for the wisdom and patience of Ingrid Beck and Pam Pugh. Thank you to the Grand Rapids community, in particular Church of the Servant, Excel Charter Academy, Jack and Carol Roeda, Rachelle Thatcher, Pam Schumaker, Leslie Christian, and Bruce Wright. Thank you to the doctors, nurses, assistants, and therapists at the rehabilitation hospital Mary Free Bed—particularly, my capable and gifted helper Ashley McKnight. Thank you to our Wheaton community, especially Elizabeth Hubbard and Micah Lindquist—two friends with joy like the sun, whose presence makes life warmer. And to Church of the Resurrection, where the beautiful presence of Jesus has been and is being made known to us. Thank you to Linda MacKillop for your wisdom and insight into the writing of my story. Thank you to my dear friends Marcus and Stacie Johnson who have borne my pain and suffering. From Toronto to Michigan to Chicago, you have been with us; to have friends here in Chicagoland who knew us during the tumult of the injury —who have cried and laughed and labored with us—is the tremendous kindness of our heavenly Father. Thank you Stacie for reading this work along the way—your authenticity and loyal support has given me courage to persevere. Thank you to our families, who provided for us in ways too many to tell. This brief acknowledgment is in no way capable of reaching the depth of our love and gratitude for the care you have shown and still provide for us. And thank you to John, William, and Gwyneth. My heart aches to think about how you each have been affected by my injury. You, more than any, bear the burdens of my pain and limitations. Thank you for your daily love and practical help. I am blessed.

Hope is eternal.

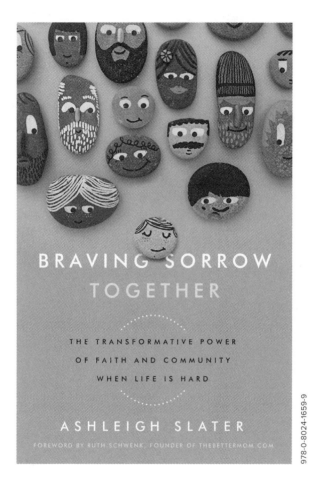

Braving Sorrow Together examines the nature of grief and loss—in relationships, health, career, and the home. It teaches us to move through trial with wisdom, releasing anxiety and receiving the help and comfort God so bountifully provides.

ALSO AVAILABLE AS AN EBOOK

Carrying baggage you don't need?

foreword by DONALD MILLER

packing light

thoughts on living life with less baggage

Allison
Vesterfelt

978-0-8024-0729-0

MOODY
Publishers®

*From the Word **to Life**®*

Packing Light is the story of Allison Vesterfelt's fifty-state road trip. Of selling her possessions and leaving a stable job. Of learning that packing light wasn't as easy as she thought. It is the story of her trip and thoughts on living life with less baggage.

ALSO AVAILABLE AS AN EBOOK

"Andy has given us all a wonderful gift—a comfort beyond human comfort and a hope beyond earthly hope."
JOHN ORTBERG

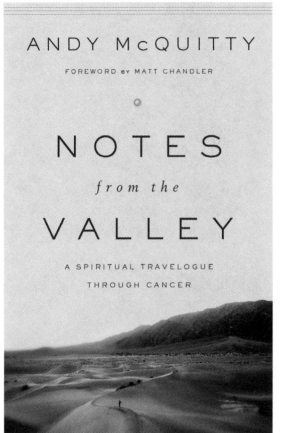

ANDY McQUITTY

FOREWORD BY MATT CHANDLER

NOTES

from the

VALLEY

A SPIRITUAL TRAVELOGUE
THROUGH CANCER

978-0-8024-1254-6

MOODY
Publishers®

From the Word to Life®

Notes from the Valley was written for anyone on the cancer journey who is craving words of God's wisdom for their journey that are simultaneously pastoral, evangelistic, theological, and, most of all, authentic.

ALSO AVAILABLE AS AN EBOOK